M É

FOR YOND

Marnie Ryan-Raison

cowandco

CONTENTS

INTRODUCTION

Macramé for Beginners and Beyond fuses the ancient art of creative knot tying with exciting new design interpretations to bring macramé into the world of modern living. Whether you are looking for an artistic feature to enliven a room, or decorative yet functional pieces to transform your entire home, we've put together a diverse selection of enticing projects to meet all your creative ambitions.

Whether you are wanting to learn a new craft or simply to advance your skills, we've something for everyone. There are twenty-four projects to choose from and we have presented them as twelve project pairings, with the first an ideal platform to begin your knotting journey and the second the perfect opportunity to expand on your current skills as a macramé artist.

In devising our designs we have aimed to introduce you to a wide variety of decorative possibilities, using an assortment of rope thicknesses, rich colourways and interesting textural techniques. There is a detailed guide to tying knots, and we strongly advise you to practise the knots you need before beginning a project.

Each project starts by listing the knots and techniques required as well as the essential materials you will need, before describing the pattern instructions in step-by-step detail for each design. There are lots of detailed photographs to guide you through the tying sequences; follow these precisely and you will see that even the most complex of designs is far easier to achieve than you might have expected.

TOOLS & MATERIALS

This section gives us the opportunity to introduce you to the most important material of all for any macramé artist, the cords for tying the knots, as well as a few basic tools that you will need. The exact materials used for each design are listed at the beginning of each project chapter.

KNOTTING CORDS

We have used a number of different cords for the projects in this book, some of which are pictured here, but the one we use most often is 5mm (¼in) rope as we find it is the perfect thickness for most projects (use too thin rope and it can become tedious and time consuming to finish projects, and thicker rope is best reserved for large scale projects only). We recommend the use of cotton rope as it is soft on the hands when knotting. Cotton rope has a much more sophisticated look than polypropylene or polyester rope, which can look tacky, and its texture is better suited to beautiful interiors.

The size and exact amounts of cord required for each project are listed at the beginning of each project. Cords may be substituted to suit your personal preference although choosing a different cord thickness will affect the quantities you require, so for the best results we suggest you limit substitutions to cord texture and colour only and we recommend that you use the same cord thickness. Cord is available through www.edeneve.com.au or from all good rope suppliers and haberdashery stores.

You may find it useful to invest in a project board for laying down your cords when working the smaller projects in the book (see Mounting Techniques). Project boards are often printed with a grid and useful basic knot-tying information, and cords are attached to the board using T-pins.

BASIC TOOLS

In addition to the tools listed in the requirements for each project, you will also need:

• Scissors

• Tape measure

• Adhesive tape

Note: When buying and cutting rope and cord lengths, use either the metric or the imperial measurements given – do not switch between the two.

KNOTS & TECHNIQUES

KNOTTING TERMINOLOGY

Before you start creating the knots, there is some basic terminology that you need to familiarize yourself with. This list covers all of the terms used in this book:

Sinnet: A vertical column of tied knots.

Row: A series of knots tied side by side.

Working cords: The cords that are used to create the knot.

Filler cords: The non-working cords around which the working cords are tied.

Holding cord: The object onto which cords are tied, that is a ring, a dowel or another piece of rope.

Alternate cords: The means by which you create a new knot by taking half of the cords from a previous knot together with half of the cords from its adjacent knot to form a new group.

OVERHAND KNOT

An overhand knot is the most basic way of tying a knot. To make a double overhand knot, simply repeat the steps.

1 Hold both ends of the cord and make a loop by bringing the left end over the right end.

2 Pull the left end through the loop and pull to secure.

HALF HITCH KNOTS

Half hitch knots are important and widely used in macramé. They are made with a working cord and holding cord, and can be used in a vertical, horizontal or diagonal manner by changing the angle of the holding cord. These instructions show you how to create various half hitch knots.

1 Begin with the working cord 2 under the holding cord 1. Bring the working cord up and over the holding cord and down through the loop. This is a *Half Hitch*.

2 Bring the working cord up and over the holding cord again, completing the *Double Half Hitch*.

3 Bring the working cord up and over the holding cord a third time to create a *Triple Half Hitch*.

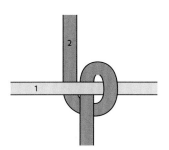
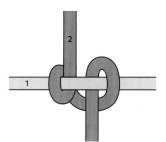
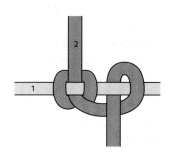

HORIZONTAL DOUBLE HALF HITCH

This is a series of double half hitches tied along a horizontal holding cord.

DIAGONAL DOUBLE HALF HITCH

This is a series of double half hitches tied along a diagonal holding cord.

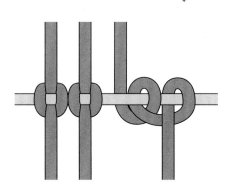
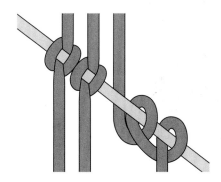

REVERSE LARK'S HEAD KNOT

The reverse lark's head knot is most commonly used as a way of mounting cords onto a piece of dowel or another horizontal holding cord.

1 Fold one length of cord in half and place it over the holding cord or dowel.

2 Bring the cord ends through the loop.

3 Pull the cord ends to secure the knot.

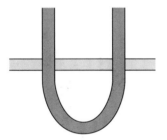
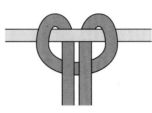

WRAPPED KNOT

A wrapped knot is generally used at the top and bottom of a hanging piece to secure the cords together.

1 Form a loop just below the cords to be wrapped, with the short end facing upwards.

2 Bring the long end back up to just below the short end and wrap firmly around all of the cords. Wrap until it reaches your desired length, ensuring that you do not cover the loop. Bring the long end down through the loop

3 Pull the short end up until the loop is about half way through the wrap. Trim the ends of the cords used to make the wrapped knot.

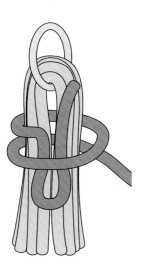

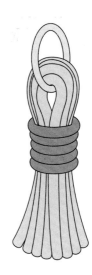

SQUARE KNOT

The square knot is one of the most commonly used macramé knots. Variations of the square knot can be achieved by using different numbers of filler cords and working cords. However, a standard square knot only uses four cords (as the diagrams shown). The basic square knot can be used to create lots of different patterns.

1 Number cords 1 to 4. The outside cords 1 and 4 are the working cords and cords 2 and 3 are the filler cords. Bring cord 1 over the filler cords and under cord 4.

2 Now bring cord 4 under the filler cords and back up between cords 1 and 2 to lay over cord 1.

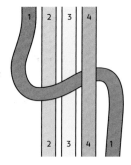

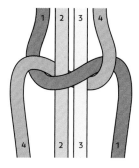

3 Bring cord 1 back over the filler cords and under cord 4.

4 Now bring cord 4 under the filler cords and back up between cords 3 and 1, and pull the working cords to tighten the knot.

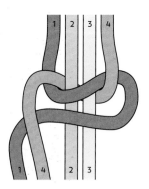

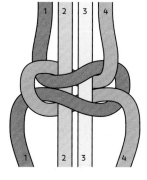

SQUARE KNOT PICOT DESIGN

This is a decorative pattern created from basic square knots.

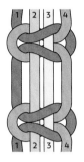

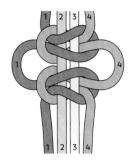

1 Tie a square knot (see Square Knot). Move down to the required area (this will be referred to in the individual pattern) and tie another square knot.

2 Slide the second knot up along the filler cords, resting it below the first knot tied.

ALTERNATING SQUARE KNOT PATTERN

The alternating square knot pattern is one of the most commonly used in macramé.

For **alternating double square knot pattern** (see advanced wall hanging), repeat each square knot row before alternating cords.

1 Tie square knots in a horizontal row (see Square Knot); for the purpose of this diagram two have been used, however this technique can be used with more square knots.

2 Alternate cords, bringing together cords 3 and 4 with cords 5 and 6, to create a square knot on a new row, using cords 3 and 6 as the working cords and cords 4 and 5 as the filler cords.

3 For the next row, tie two square knots as in step 1, with cords 1–4 for the first square knot and cords 5–8 for the second square knot.

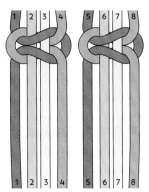

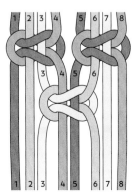

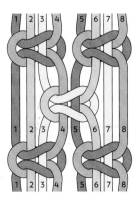

INCREASING SQUARE KNOT PATTERN

Starting with a single square knot row, the number of square knots tied increases by one in each consecutive row. For the diagrams as shown, the increasing square knot pattern has been worked using twelve cords (finishing with three square knots); however, fewer or more cords may be used (this will be referred to in the individual pattern).

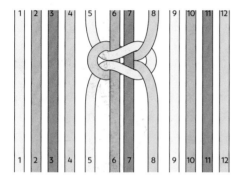

1 Number the cords 1 to 12. Tie a square knot (see Square Knot) with cords 5–8.

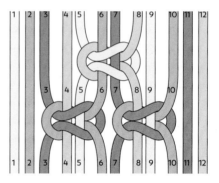

2 Tie the second row of square knots with cords 3–6 and 7–10.

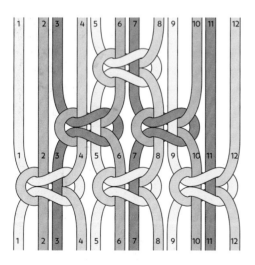

3 Tie the third row of square knots with cords 1–4, 5–8 and 9–12.

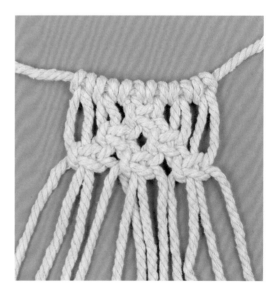

DECREASING SQUARE KNOT PATTERN

With this pattern, the amount of square knots tied in each consecutive row decreases. For the diagrams as shown, the decreasing square knot pattern has been worked using twelve cords (beginning with three square knots); however, fewer or more cords may be used (this will be referred to in the individual pattern).

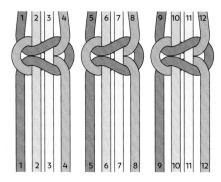

1 Tie a row of square knots (see Square Knot) with cords 1–4, 5–8 and 9–12.

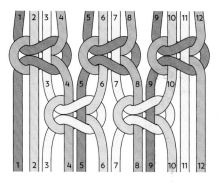

2 Tie the second row of square knots with cords 3–6 and 7 10.

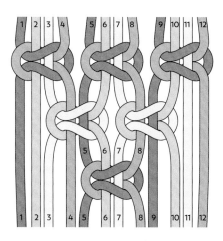

3 Tie the third row of square knots with cords 5–8.

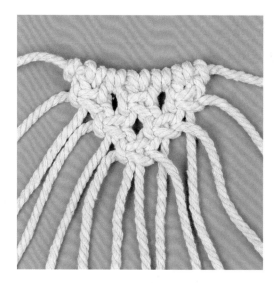

HALF KNOT

A half knot is basically half a square knot. Half knots can be tied in rows and worked to create an alternating pattern, too.

1 Number cords 1 to 4. The outside cords 1 and 4 are the working cords and cords 2 and 3 are the filler cords. Bring cord 1 over the filler cords and under cord 4.

2 Now bring cord 4 under the filler cords and back up between cords 1 and 2 to lay over cord 1.

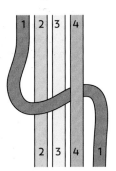

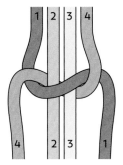

Half knots can be worked in an ***alternating half knot pattern*** in the same way that square knots can be worked in an alternating square knot pattern (see Square Knots: Alternating Square Knot Pattern). The table mat project is made with an alternating half knot pattern.

HALF KNOT SPIRAL

The half knot spiral is a sinnet (vertical column) made with half knots, which naturally twist as you continue to tie them. You can help to create a uniform look by deliberately rotating and tightening the knots at regular intervals.

1 Number cords 1 to 4. The outside cords 1 and 4 are the working cords and cords 2 and 3 are the filler cords. Bring cord 1 over the filler cords and under cord 4.

2 Now bring cord 4 under the filler cords and up between cords 1 and 2 to lay over cord 1.

3 Continue to repeat steps 1 and 2 as many times as instructed in the individual pattern to create a half knot spiral.

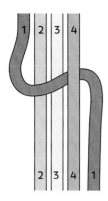

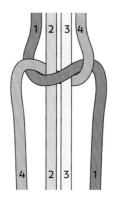

CHINESE CROWN KNOT

To tie a Chinese crown knot you'll need to place the cords upside down on your lap and secure them in place between your knees. The single cords shown in the diagrams and photo sample represent cord groups of several cords.

1 Divide the cords into four equal groups and place the cord groups in their allocated positions, with cord groups labelled 1 to 4 and the spaces in between the cord groups labelled A to D.

2 Place cord group 1 into space A, ensuring that there is a loop at the fold.

3 Place cord group 2 over cord group 1 and into space B. Bring cord group 2 all the way into the centre (see step 4) and do not leave a loop.

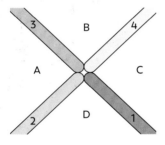

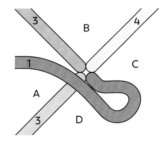

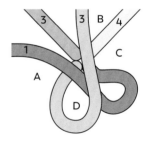

4 Place cord group 3 over cord groups 2 and 4 and under the loop into space C.

5 Place cord group 4 through the loop bringing it into space D.

6 Pull all cord groups together evenly until the knot is formed.

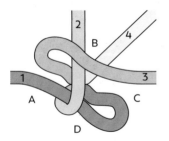

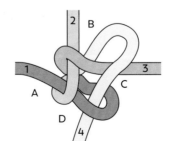

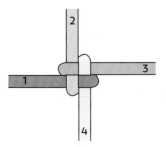

TECHNIQUES

There are a few basic techniques that you will need to complete the projects in this book and these are explained here.

MOUNTING TECHNIQUES

It is important to achieve a firm tension when tying your knots, so you need to set yourself up before you get underway, following the advice below.

For small projects, such as the clutch purse, where you use rope as your holding cord, or when making finer items such as jewellery, a project board and T-pins are particularly useful (see Tools & Materials). Alternatively, mount your holding cord to a board, wall or other flat surface, and secure it with adhesive tape.

For wall hangings or plant hangers, where you use a dowel or a metal ring to mount your cords from, a clothes rack becomes a great work station. Simply tie your dowel or metal ring to the horizontal rail of the clothes rack or use S-hooks to secure these holding cords in place. Alternatively, use a single wall hook to hang a metal ring from when making a plant hanger, or two wall hooks to rest a piece of dowel onto when making a wall hanging.

For large width projects, such as our celebration arch, you can suspend your dowel from a curtain rod or two strong wall hooks, but do be aware of the weight-bearing capacity of the wall hooks.

For projects with a long vertical holding cord, such as the hanging light or indoor swing, you can use a hook anchored into a ceiling beam to suspend your working project from, but do make sure that the weight-bearing capacity of the hook is appropriate to your project.

WRAPPING A RING

Take your length of rope and secure one end of it onto the metal ring by tying a double half hitch (see Half Hitch Knots). Taking the long end of the cord through the ring, wrap the rope around the ring to cover it completely leaving just enough space to secure it to the ring with another double half hitch. Trim any excess cord.

FRAYING

This is a finishing technique where the rope is unravelled by separating each strand into its constituent parts to create a fringing effect or for a fuller tassel.

WEAVING FINISH

A finishing technique where the ends of the rope are woven underneath the knots on the back of the design for a neat finish.

PLAITING

Plaiting is the interlacing of three cords or groups of cords to create a braid. Cross the left-hand cord over the centre cord to become the centre cord. Then cross the right-hand cord over the new centre cord so that it now takes the centre position. Continue to alternate left- and right-hand cords to the centre position to form the braid.

NUMBERING CORDS

This is a way of counting cords to find the exact section to begin working from in a macramé pattern. Cords are counted from left to right; for smaller projects where fewer cords are used, this can be done mentally. When working on large projects that use many cords to create the pattern, the celebration arch for example, it is easy to lose count. To help you to keep track, you can temporarily tie a piece of bright yarn around every tenth cord, or you can use pegs to keep groups of cords together.

LACING UP

The sides of the pocket on the clutch purse are laced together by threading the holding cord through the spaces in the alternating square knot patterns.

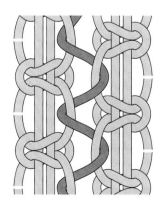

PROJECTS

HANGING SHELF

This decorative shelf unit is ideal for displaying light objects. Perfect for any room in your home, it is suspended from a 16-cord half knot spiral and it can be hung either from the wall or from the ceiling against a wall, but do be sure to insert a wall plug and screw with a minimum 10kg (22lb) load. Please note: the type of plug and screw required will depend on your wall structure and the weight of the shelves and the items to be displayed.

MATERIALS:

- 74m (242½ft) length of 5mm (¼in) rope
- 8cm (3⅛in) metal ring
- Two pieces of pine wood each measuring 48cm (19in) long x 18.5cm (7¼in) wide x 2cm (¾in) thick
- Drill with 15mm (¹⁹⁄₃₂in) diameter wood drill bit
- 120 grit (fine) sandpaper
- Wood stain in your preferred colour

KNOTS & TECHNIQUES:

- Half Knot Spiral
- Overhand Knot
- Wrapping a Ring
- Mounting Techniques
- Fraying

PREPARATION:

- Cut eight 9m (29½ft) lengths of 5mm (¼in) rope
- Cut one 2m (6½ft) length of 5mm (¼in) rope
- At each corner of each of the wood pieces, mark a hole position 2cm (¾in) from the sides, then drill the holes
- Lightly sand the wood to remove any rough or uneven surfaces, then stain to your desired colour

Method

1 Wrap the 8cm (3⅛in) metal ring with the 2m (6½ft) length of rope (see Wrapping a Ring).

2 Mount the eight 9m (29½ft) lengths of rope onto the ring by folding them in half over the inside of the ring. (See Mounting Techniques for preparing to start.)

3 Separate the cords into three consecutive groups: group 1 – four cords; group 2 – eight cords; and group 3 – four cords.

4 Using group 1 and group 3 cords as the working cords and group 2 as the filler cords (see Knotting Terminology), tie a 16-cord half knot spiral with eight half knots (see Half Knot Spiral).

5 Now separate the cords into four groups of four cords.

6 Drop down 1.5cm (⅝in) and tie a 4-cord half knot spiral with sixty-four half knots for each of the four groups.

7 Place your first shelf horizontally and thread the four cords from each of the half knot spirals through each of the drilled corner holes.

8 Turn the shelf upside down and tie each group of cords with an overhand knot (see Overhand Knot) to secure the shelf in place at each corner. Once all four knots have been tied, turn the shelf right way up and make sure it is level before continuing.

9 Directly beneath each overhand knot tie a 4-cord half knot spiral with thirty-two half knots for each of your four groups of cords.

10 Repeat steps 7 and 8.

11 Trim the cords to 5.5cm (2¼in) and fray (see Fraying).

HANGING TABLE

Give your living area a unique focal point with this truly amazing hanging table. While it can be used to display lighter ornaments, all eyes will be on the macramé itself. The hanging 'chain' is created from Chinese crown knots, and a beautiful square knot picot design has been used for the hanging straps. Please note: to hang the table, a hook must be inserted into a ceiling beam with a minimum weight-bearing capacity of 10kg (22lb).

MATERIALS:

- 147m (482ft) length of 5mm (¼in) rope

- Metal rings: one 6cm (2⅜in); one 9cm (3½in)

- 30cm (1ft) length of 2.5mm (⅛in) cotton twine

- 40–60cm (15⅝–23½in) circular tray of your choice

KNOTS & TECHNIQUES:

- Wrapped Knot

- Chinese Crown Knot

- Double Half Hitch

- Square Knot

- Alternating Square Knot Pattern

- Square Knot Picot Design

- Overhand Knot

- Fraying

PREPARATION:

- Cut sixteen 9m (29½ft) lengths of 5mm (¼in) rope

- Cut two 1.5m (5ft) lengths of 5mm (¼in) rope

Method

1 Mount the sixteen 9m (29½ft) lengths of rope onto the 6cm (2⅜in) metal ring by folding them in half over the inside of the ring.

2 Using a 1.5m (5ft) length of rope, secure the cords together with a 5cm (2in) wrapped knot (see Wrapped Knot).

3 Separate the cords into four groups of eight cords and tie six Chinese crown knots (see Chinese Crown Knot).

4 Directly beneath the Chinese crown knots, place all the cords inside the 9cm (3½in) metal ring. The metal ring sitting horizontally is now to be used as the holding cord (see Knotting Terminology). Keeping the ring level at all times, tie double half hitches (see Half Hitch Knots) with all cords onto the ring.

5 Secure the ring in place by tying a row of eight square knots (see Square Knot) directly beneath the ring.

6 Separate the cords into four groups of eight cords. Each group now becomes a sinnet (see Knotting Terminology). Repeat steps 7–14 for each sinnet.

7 Tie eight rows of alternating square knots (see Alternating Square Knot Pattern).

8 Drop down 5cm (2in) and tie a square knot using four filler cords and two working cords on either side. This is an 8-cord square knot (see Square Knot).

9 Drop down 3cm (1⅛in) and tie another 8-cord square knot.

10 Drop down 3cm (1⅛in) and tie another 8-cord square knot.

11 Slide the square knots up the filler cords to create a square knot picot design (see Square Knot Picot Design).

12 Drop down 5cm (2in) and tie three rows of alternating square knots.

13 Repeat steps 8–11.

14 Drop down 27cm (10⅝in) and tie nine rows of alternating square knots.

15 Alternate cords (see Knotting Terminology) by taking four cords from each adjacent sinnet and bringing them together. Drop down 22cm (8⅝in) and tie an 8-cord square knot (so that each sinnet is joined to the one next to it with an 8-cord square knot).

16 Drop down 7cm (2¾in), gather all cords together and use the 30cm (1ft) length of cotton twine to tie a double overhand knot (see Overhand Knot).

17 Cover the overhand knot with a 5cm (2in) wrapped knot using the remaining 1.5m (5ft) length of rope.

18 Trim the cords to the desired length and fray (see Fraying).

19 Insert the circular tray to create the table top.

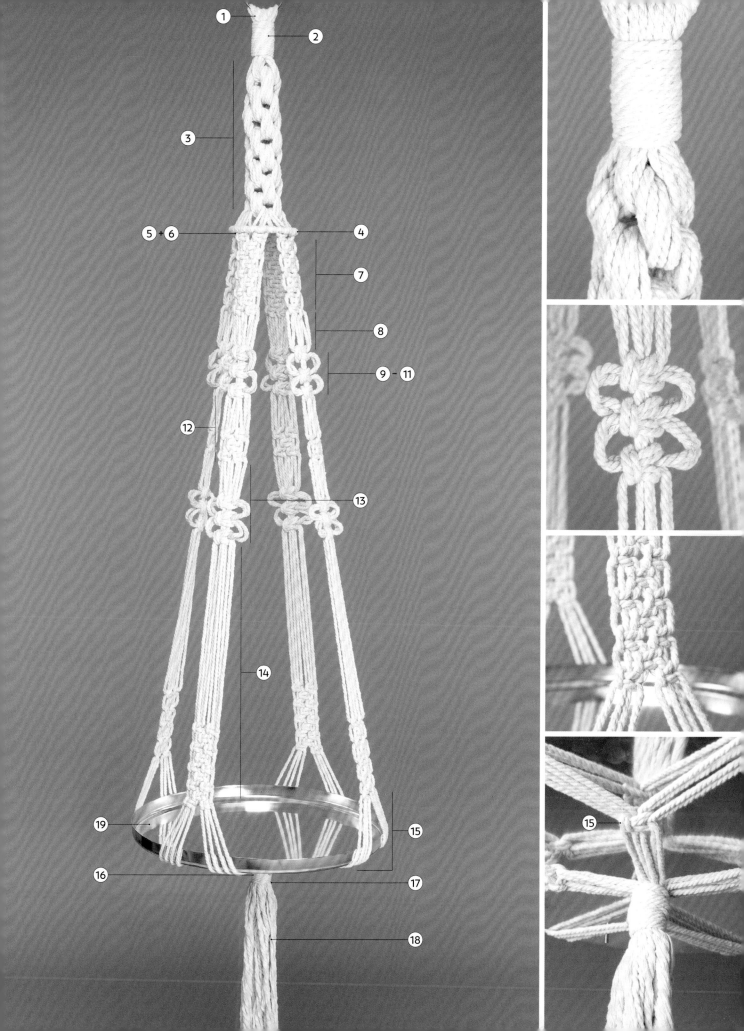

BOTTLE HOLDER

● ● ●

MATERIALS:

- 44.3m (146¼ft) length of 2mm (³⁄₃₂in) jute

- Glass jar measuring 26cm (10¼in) high with an 8cm (3⅛in) diameter base

KNOTS & TECHNIQUES:

- Chinese Crown Knot

- Square Knot

- Overhand Knot

- Wrapped Knot

- Plaiting

Perfect for storing a special bottle of wine, this beautiful holder could also be used to showcase your favourite glass vase, and it could even double up as a plant hanger. It has rustic plaited hanging straps and a sturdy wrapped handle. Made with jute, this piece perfectly complements an interior design scheme inspired by natural, earthy colours.

PREPARATION:

- Cut sixteen 2.5m (8¼ft) lengths of 2mm (³⁄₃₂in) jute

- Cut one 4m (13¼ft) length of 2mm (³⁄₃₂in) jute

- Cut one 30cm (1ft) length of 2mm (³⁄₃₂in) jute

Method

1   Divide the sixteen 2.5m (8¼ft) lengths of jute into two groups of eight cords and lay each group down on a flat surface so that they cross over at the centre.

2   Tie a Chinese crown knot to secure the two groups of cord together (see Chinese Crown Knot). You now have four bundles of cord radiating out from the Chinese crown knot centre – this is the start of the base of the bottle holder.

3   Bring four cords from one bundle together with four cords from its adjacent bundle so you have a group of eight cords. Drop down 3cm (1⅛in) from the middle of the Chinese crown knot and tie an 8-cord square knot (see Square Knot) using four filler cords and two working cords (see Knotting Terminology) on either side.

4   Repeat step 3 until you have a total of four 8-cord square knots around the centre point.

5   Alternate cords as in step 3, leave a gap of 3cm (1⅛in) and tie another row of four 8-cord square knots.

6   Continuing to alternate cords and leaving 3cm (1⅛in) gaps in between each row, create six more rows of 8-cord square knots. (Once a cup-like shape begins to form, which should happen by about the third row, you can turn your glass jar upside down, place your cords over it and continue tying.)

7   Bring eight cords from one 8-cord square knot together with eight cords from the one adjacent to it. Drop down 3cm (1⅛in) and tie a 16-cord square knot using eight filler cords and four working cords on either side.

8   Repeat step 7 on the remaining two 8-cord square knots.

9   You now have two 16-cord square knots, one on either side of the design and these are the starting points for making the hanging straps. Working on one of the 16-cord square knots, separate the sixteen cords into groups of five, five and six cords and work a tight plait 30cm (1ft) long (see Plaiting). Plait the cords from the second 16-cord square knot in the same way.

10 To start to make the handle, overlap the ends of the plaited straps by 5cm (2in), making sure that one sits flat on top of the other. Gather together all cords and use the 30cm (1ft) length of jute to firmly tie a double overhand knot (see Overhand Knot) at the centre of the overlapping straps.

11 Using the remaining 4m (13¼ft) length of jute, tie a wrapped knot 14cm (5½in) long (see Wrapped Knot) to cover the double overhand knot, which should be at the centre of the wrapped knot. Trim off all excess cords.

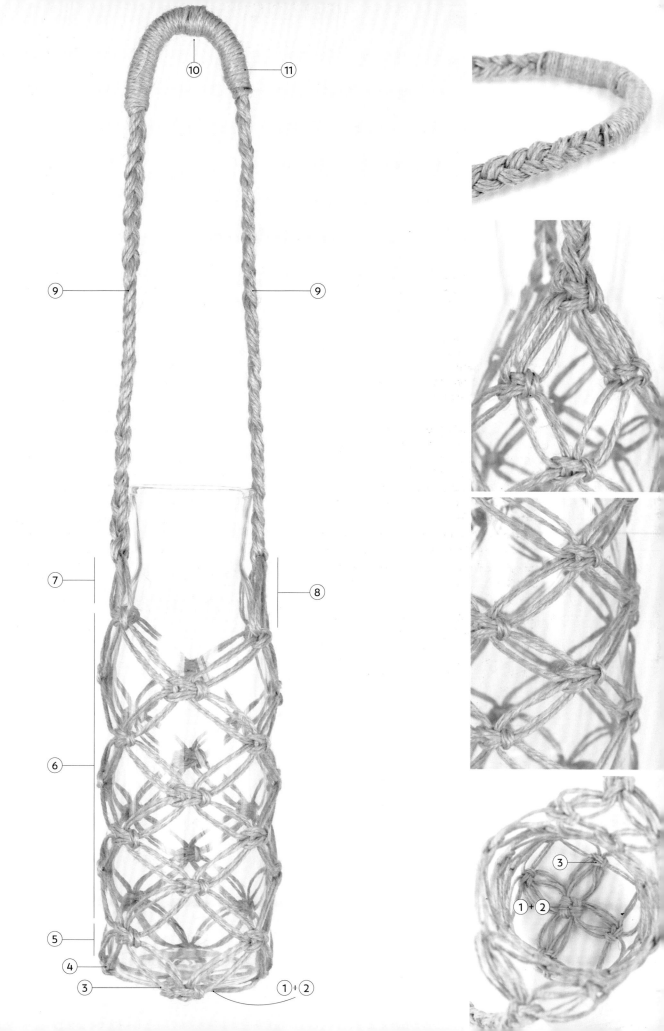

HANGING BASKET

• • •

MATERIALS:

- 167m (553ft) length of 2.5mm (⅛in) rope
- 6cm (2⅜in) metal ring
- Two 20cm (7⅞in) cane rings

KNOTS & TECHNIQUES:

- Wrapped Knot
- Square Knot
- Triple Half Hitch
- Alternating Square Knot Pattern
- Overhand Knot
- Wrapping a Ring
- Mounting Techniques

This basket-style hanger is a multi-functional piece that is equally at home when used as a plant hanger in the conservatory, as a craft caddy in your sewing room, or as a hanging fruit bowl in the kitchen. Alternating square knots create a beautiful net-like pattern for the basket enclosure.

PREPARATION:

- Cut forty 4m (13¼ft) lengths of 2.5mm (⅛in) rope
- Cut three 2m (6½ft) lengths of 2.5mm (⅛in) rope
- Cut one 1m (3¼ft) length of 2.5mm (⅛in) rope

Method

1 Wrap the 6cm (2⅜in) metal ring with a 2m (6½ft) length of rope (see Wrapping a Ring).

2 Mount the forty 4m (13⅛ft) lengths of rope onto the ring by folding them in half over the inside of the ring. (See Mounting Techniques for preparing to start.)

3 Using one of the 2m (6½ft) lengths of rope, secure all cords together directly under the ring using a 3.5cm (1⅜in) wrapped knot (see Wrapped Knot).

4 Directly under the wrapped knot, separate the cords into eight groups of ten cords. Each group will now become a sinnet (see Knotting Terminology). Repeat steps 5–8 for each sinnet.

5 Tie four 10-cord square knots using four filler cords and three working cords on each side (see Square Knot).

6 Drop down 17cm (6¾in) and use the middle six cords to tie one 6-cord square knot using four filler cords and one working cord on each side.

7 Directly beneath, alternate cords (see Knotting Terminology) and tie two 5-cord square knots using three filler cords and one working cord on each side.

8 Directly beneath, use the middle six cords to tie another 6-cord square knot, using four filler cords and one working cord on each side.

9 Drop down 17cm (6¾in) and place all of the cords inside the first of your cane rings. The cane ring sitting horizontally is now to be used as the holding cord (see Knotting Terminology). Tie triple half hitches (see Half Hitch Knots) with each cord onto the cane ring.

10 Secure the first cane ring by tying a row of twenty square knots directly beneath the ring.

11 Drop down 1.5cm (⅝in), alternate cords and tie another row of twenty square knots.

12 Continue an alternating square knot pattern for another eight rows (see Alternating Square Knot Pattern).

13 Place all cords inside the second cane ring. The cane ring sitting horizontally is now to be used as the holding cord. Tie triple half hitches with each cord onto the cane ring.

14 Gather the rope firmly and bring it upwards until it is centred and level with the cane ring. This will create a base for the hanging basket. Secure with a double overhand knot (see Overhand Knot) using the 1m (3¼ft) length of rope.

15 Using the remaining 2m (6½ft) length of rope, tie a 3.5cm (1⅜in) wrapped knot over the top of the double overhand knot.

16 Trim the cords to the desired length.

TABLE MAT

MATERIALS:

• 82.1m (272ft) length of 5mm (¼in) rope

KNOTS & TECHNIQUES:

• Horizontal Double Half Hitch

• Half Knot

• Overhand Knot

• Mounting Techniques

• Fraying

From family breakfasts to dinner dates with friends, this macramé table mat has a simple elegance that is sure to impress. Use just one to showcase your table centre piece or make a set for stylish placemats. The alternating half knot pattern creates a dense fabric to keep your table top protected and when made with cotton rope, these mats can be hand-washed.

PREPARATION:

• Cut thirty-six 2.25m (7½ft) lengths of 5mm (¼in) rope

• Cut two 55cm (22in) lengths of 5mm (¼in) rope

Method

1   Secure one of the 55cm (22in) rope lengths to a project board using T-pins, or to a flat surface with adhesive tape. (See Mounting Techniques for preparing to start.) This becomes your holding cord (see Knotting Terminology).

2   Mount the thirty-six 2.25m (7½ft) lengths of rope onto the holding cord using horizontal double half hitches (see Half Hitch Knots), leaving cord ends 10cm (4in) above your holding cord to make the fringe.

3   Directly beneath the row of double half hitches, tie a row of nine half knots (see Half Knot).

4   Alternate cords (see Knotting Terminology) and tie another row of eight half knots.

5   Alternate cords and tie a row of nine half knots.

6   Continue an alternating half knot pattern for a further forty-eight rows.

7   Directly beneath the last row of half knots and on top of all cords, place the remaining 55cm (22in) length of rope to create a second holding cord. Tie all cords onto the second holding cord with horizontal double half hitches.

8   Tie an overhand knot (see Overhand Knot) at each end of the two holding cords.

9   Trim all cords to 5cm (2in) and fray (see Fraying) to make a fringe at either end of the mat.

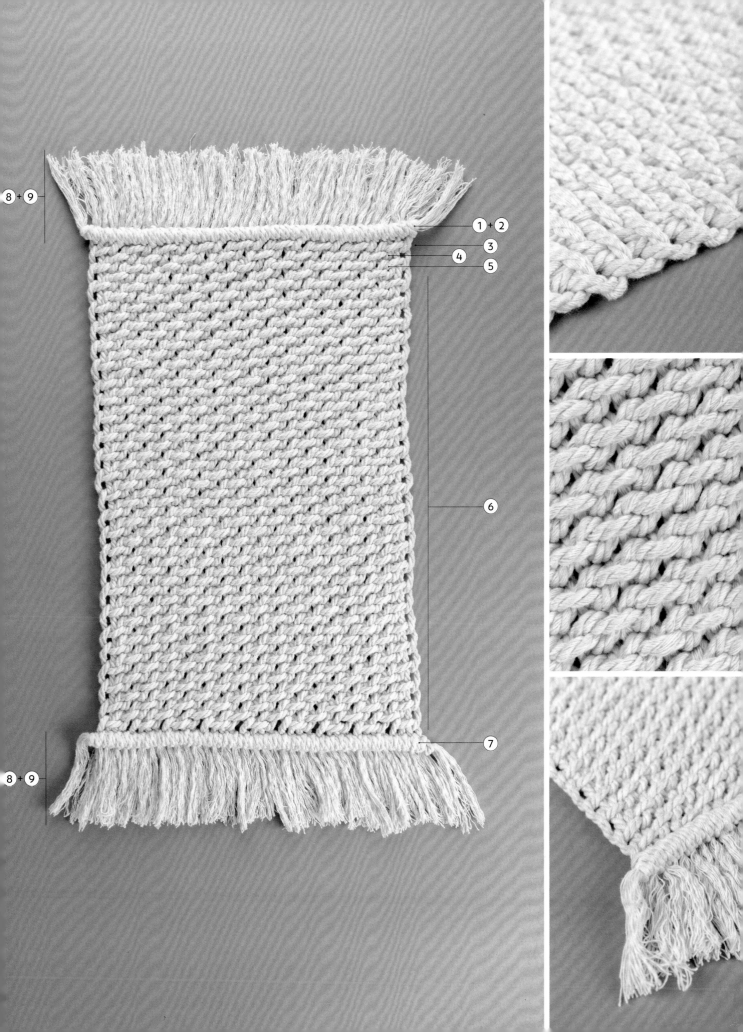

TABLE RUNNER

MATERIALS:

- 208m (682½ft) length of 5mm (¼in) rope
- 50cm (20in) length of 2.5cm (1in) dowel

KNOTS & TECHNIQUES:

- Reverse Lark's Head Knot
- Square Knot
- Half Knot
- Alternating Square Knot Pattern
- Increasing Square Knot Pattern
- Decreasing Square Knot Pattern
- Mounting Techniques
- Numbering Cords

This table runner makes a beautiful statement piece to show off your table setting, for everyday family dinners to special occasion entertaining, such as weddings. The centre diamond design is made with an increasing and decreasing square knot pattern, and the side panels can easily be worked longer to match the size of your table. When made with cotton rope the table runner can be hand-washed or simply spot cleaned.

PREPARATION:

- Cut twenty-six 8m (26¼ft) lengths of 5mm (¼in) rope

Method

1 Mount all twenty-six 8m (26¼ft) lengths of rope onto the dowel using reverse lark's head knots (see Reverse Lark's Head Knot) ensuring that the rope lengths are evenly spaced apart. The width of the mounted rope should be 36cm (14⅛in). (See Mounting Techniques for preparing to start.)

2 Drop down 10cm (4in) and tie a row of thirteen square knots (see Square Knot).

3 Directly beneath the row of square knots, alternate cords (see Knotting Terminology) and tie a row of twelve half knots (see Half Knot).

4 Alternate cords and tie a row of thirteen half knots.

5 Alternate cords and tie a row of twelve half knots.

6 Directly beneath, tie a row of thirteen square knots.

7 Alternate cords, drop down 3cm (1⅛in) and tie a row of twelve square knots.

8 Continue an alternating square knot pattern (see Alternating Square Knot Pattern) with 3cm (1⅛in) gaps for another three rows.

9 Repeat steps 3–6.

10 Number the cords 1 to 52 (see Numbering Cords).

11 Working with cords 1–4, drop down 3cm (1⅛in) and tie a square knot. These cords will now become a sinnet (see Knotting Terminology). Tie six more square knots with gaps of 3cm (1⅛in) in between.

12 Working with cords 49–52 this time, repeat step 11.

13 Gather cords 25–28, drop down 3cm (1⅛in) and tie a square knot.

14 Beginning with the square knot created with cords 25–28 in step 13, begin to work an increasing square knot pattern (see Increasing Square Knot Pattern), tying the rows directly beneath one another. Continue the increasing square knot pattern until you have completed a row of eleven square knots: this is the last row of the increasing square knot pattern.

15 Directly beneath the row of eleven square knots, begin a decreasing square knot pattern (see Decreasing Square Knot Pattern) until you have completed the last row of just one square knot.

16 Drop down 3cm (1⅛in) and tie a row of thirteen square knots.

17 Repeat steps 3–8.

18 Repeat steps 3–6.

19 Trim the cord ends to 12cm (4¾in) below the last row of square knots.

20 Carefully slip the mounted rope off the dowel. Unfold the reverse lark's head knots and cut the cords at the fold. Trim the cord ends if necessary to match the fringe at the other end of the runner.

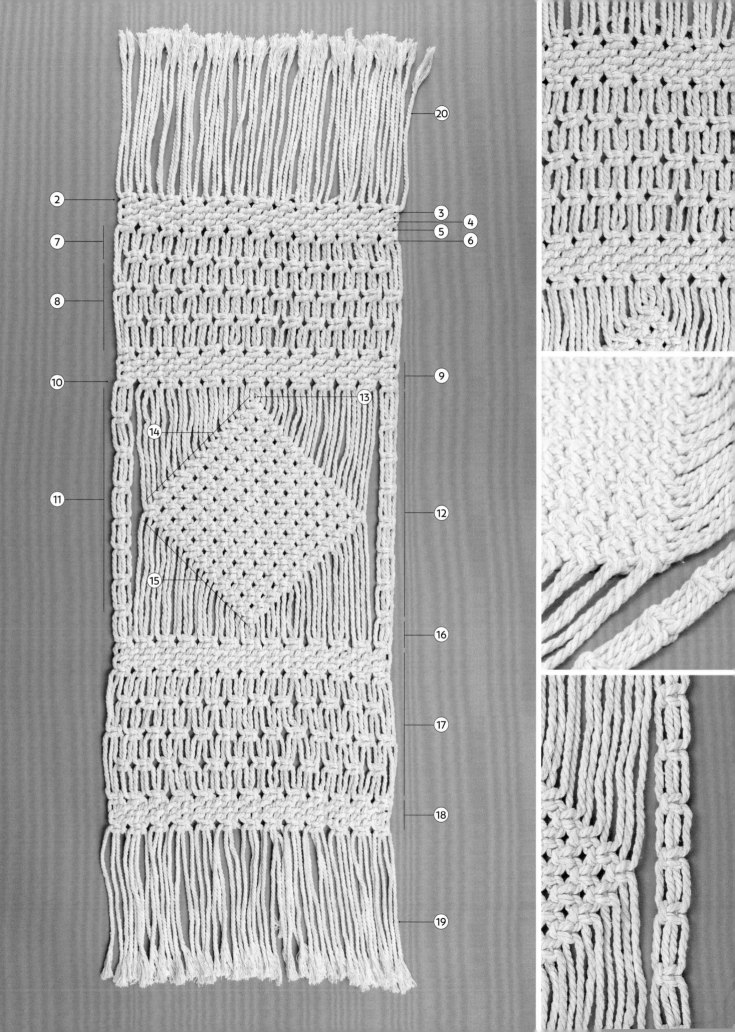

BASIC WALL HANGING

MATERIALS:

- 56m (184ft) length of 5mm (¼in) rope
- 28cm (11in) length of 2.5cm (1in) dowel

KNOTS & TECHNIQUES:

- Reverse Lark's Head Knot
- Square Knot
- Alternating Square Knot Pattern
- Decreasing Square Knot Pattern
- Mounting Techniques
- Fraying

This simple, decorative wall hanging, made with natural cotton rope, will perfectly complement any space in the modern home. If you are new to macramé, this is a great starter project to learn the popular square knot and alternating square knot pattern. You could easily swap the piece of dowel for some foraged driftwood if you wanted a more earthy look.

PREPARATION:

- Cut sixteen 3.5m (11½ft) lengths of 5mm (¼in) rope

Method

1 Mount the sixteen 3.5m (11½ft) lengths of rope onto the dowel using reverse lark's head knots (see Reverse Lark's Head Knot). The width of the mounted rope should be 22cm (8⅝in), with 3cm (1⅛in) left uncovered at each end of the dowel. (See Mounting Techniques for preparing to start.)

2 Directly beneath the dowel, tie a row of eight square knots (see Square Knot).

3 Working directly beneath each row, tie twenty-two rows of alternating square knot pattern (see Alternating Square Knot Pattern).

4 Now start to work rows of decreasing square knot pattern (see Decreasing Square Knot Pattern), starting with a row of seven square knots and finishing with a single square knot.

5 Trim the cords so that they are even and fray if desired (see Fraying).

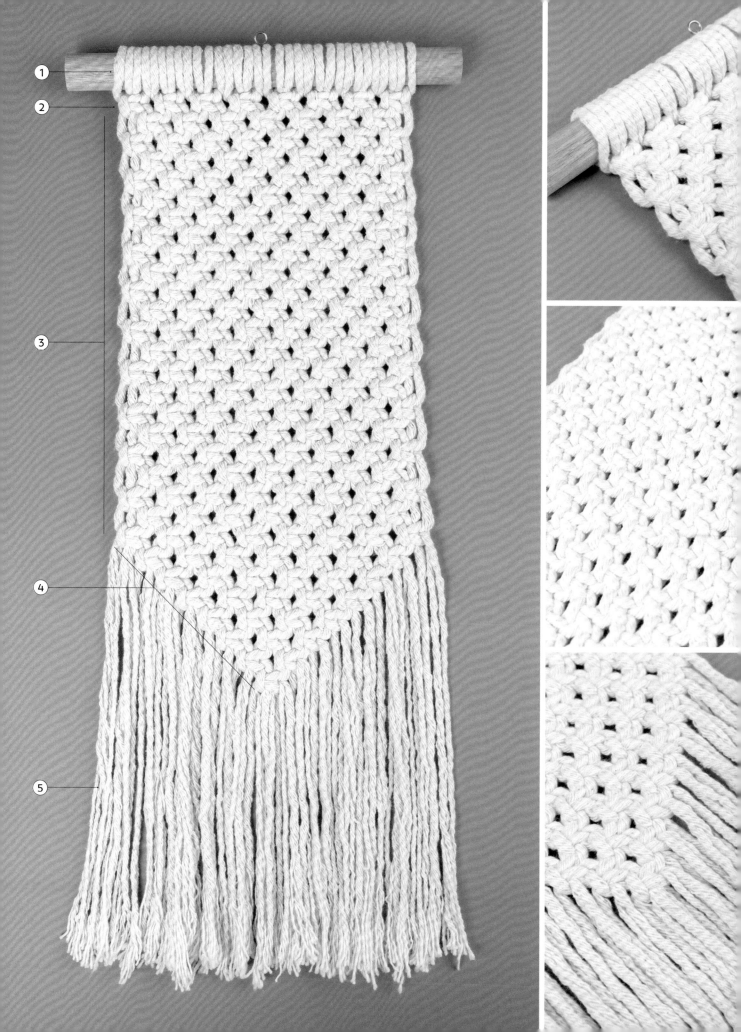

ADVANCED WALL HANGING

A retro inspired and geometric styled wall hanging that is sure to impress as it showcases your developing skills. Ideal for an intermediate level, it demonstrates how by combining a few of the basic macramé knots, a unique and intricately knotted pattern can be created. The top and bottom panels are worked with an alternating double square knot pattern and are joined by a feature arrow design and a band of half knot spirals.

MATERIALS:

- 136m (448½ft) length of 5mm (¼in) rope
- 46cm (18¼in) length of 1.8cm (¾in) dowel

KNOTS & TECHNIQUES:

- Reverse Lark's Head Knot
- Square Knot
- Alternating Double Square Knot Pattern
- Horizontal Double Half Hitch
- Overhand Knot
- Diagonal Double Half Hitch
- Half Knot Spiral
- Mounting Techniques
- Fraying
- Numbering Cords

PREPARATION:

- Cut twenty-six 5m (16½ft) lengths of 5mm (¼in) rope
- Cut four 1m (3¼ft) lengths of 5mm (¼in) rope
- Cut one 2m (6½ft) length of 5mm (¼in) rope

Method

1   Mount all twenty-six 5m (16½ft) lengths of rope onto the dowel using reverse lark's head knots (see Reverse Lark's Head Knot). The width of the mounted rope should be 39cm (15¼in), with 3.5cm (1⅜in) left uncovered at each end of the dowel. (See Mounting Techniques for preparing to start.)

2   Directly beneath the dowel, tie a row of thirteen square knots (see Square Knot).

3   Tie another row of thirteen square knots directly beneath the previous row.

4   Alternate cords (see Knotting Terminology) and tie a row of twelve square knots.

5   Tie another row of twelve square knots directly beneath the previous row.

6   Alternate cords and tie a row of thirteen square knots directly beneath the previous row.

7   Repeat step 3 to complete the first panel of alternating double square knot pattern (see Alternating Square Knot Pattern).

8   Place a 1m (3¼ft) length of rope horizontally directly beneath the last row of knots. This is now the holding cord (see Knotting Terminology).

9   Tie horizontal double half hitches (see Half Hitch Knots) with all cords along the holding cord.

10 Tie an overhand knot (see Overhand Knot) at each end of the holding cord and trim the ends to 10cm (4in) and fray (see Fraying).

11 Tie a row of thirteen square knots.

12 Now start to create the arrow design panel (steps 12–48). First, number the cords 1 to 52 (see Numbering Cords).

13 Make cord 3 a holding cord (see Knotting Terminology); bring it down left to right and tie diagonal double half hitches (see Half Hitch Knots) with cords 4–8.

14 Make cord 14 a holding cord; bring it down right to left and tie diagonal double half hitches with cords 9–13.

15 Make cord 15 a holding cord; bring it down left to right and tie diagonal double half hitches with cords 16–20.

16 Make cord 26 a holding cord; bring it down right to left and tie diagonal double half hitches with cords 21–25.

17 Make cord 27 a holding cord; bring it down left to right and tie diagonal double half hitches with cords 28–32.

18 Make cord 38 a holding cord; bring it down right to left and tie diagonal double half hitches with cords 33–37.

19 Make cord 39 a holding cord; bring it down left to right and tie diagonal double half hitches with cords 40–44.

20 Make cord 50 a holding cord; bring it down right to left and tie diagonal double half hitches with cords 45–49.

21 Number the cords 1 to 52.

22 Make cord 2 a holding cord; bring it down left to right and tie diagonal double half hitches with cords 3–7.

23 Make cord 14 a holding cord; bring it down right to left and tie diagonal double half hitches with cords 10–13.

24 Make cord 15 a holding cord; bring it down left to right and tie diagonal double half hitches with cords 16–19.

25 Make cord 26 a holding cord; bring it down right to left and tie diagonal double half hitches with cords 22–25.

26 Make cord 27 a holding cord; bring it down left to right and tie diagonal double half hitches with cords 28–31.

27 Make cord 38 a holding cord; bring it down right to left and tie diagonal double half hitches with cords 34–37.

28 Make cord 39 a holding cord; bring it down left to right and tie diagonal double half hitches with cords 40–43.

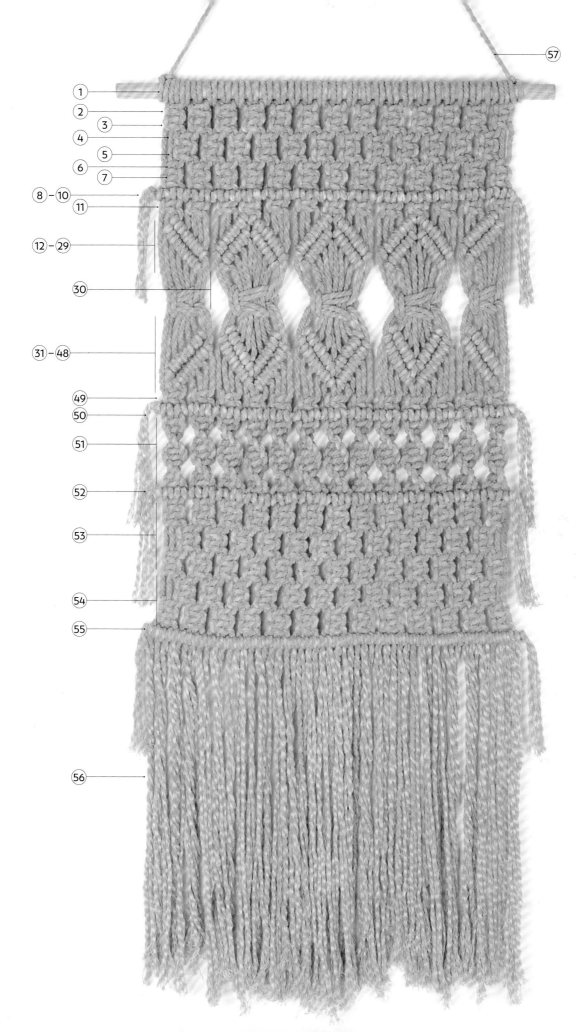

29 Make cord 51 a holding cord; bring it down right to left and tie diagonal double half hitches with cords 46–50.

30 Drop down 1cm (⅜in) and tie a row of five square knots (see Square Knot) as follows: the first square knot consists of two working cords on each side and four filler cords; the second, third and fourth square knots consist of two working cords on each side and eight filler cords; and the fifth square knot consists of two working cords on each side and four filler cords.

31 Number cords 1 to 52.

32 Make cord 7 a holding cord; bring it down right to left and tie diagonal double half hitches with cords 2–6.

33 Make cord 10 a holding cord; bring it down left to right and tie diagonal double half hitches with cords 11–14.

34 Make cord 19 a holding cord; bring it down right to left and tie diagonal double half hitches with cords 15–18.

35 Make cord 22 a holding cord; bring it down left to right and tie diagonal double half hitches with cords 23–26.

36 Make cord 31 a holding cord; bring it down right to left and tie diagonal double half hitches with cords 27–30.

37 Make cord 34 a holding cord; bring it down left to right and tie diagonal double half hitches with cords 35–38.

38 Make cord 43 a holding cord; bring it down right to left and tie diagonal double half hitches with cords 39–42.

39 Make cord 46 a holding cord; bring it down left to right and tie diagonal double half hitches with cords 47–51.

40 Number cords 1 to 52.

41 Make cord 8 a holding cord; bring it down right to left and tie diagonal double half hitches with cords 3–7.

42 Make cord 9 a holding cord; bring it down left to right and tie diagonal double half hitches with cords 10–14.

43 Make cord 20 a holding cord; bring it down right to left and tie diagonal double half hitches with cords 15–19.

44 Make cord 21 a holding cord; bring it down left to right and tie diagonal double half hitches with cords 22–26.

45 Make cord 32 a holding cord; bring it down right to left and tie diagonal double half hitches with cords 27–31.

46 Make cord 33 a holding cord; bring it down left to right and tie diagonal double half hitches with cords 34–38.

47 Make cord 44 a holding cord; bring it down right to left and tie diagonal double half hitches with cords 39–43.

48 Make cord 45 a holding cord; bring it down left to right and tie diagonal double half hitches with cords 46–50.

49 Tie a row of thirteen square knots directly beneath.

50 Repeat steps 8, 9 and 10 using a second 1m (3¼ft) length of rope as the holding cord.

51 Directly beneath, begin a row of ten half knot spirals (see Half Knot Spiral), made by tying thirteen half knots for each of the sinnets (see Knotting Terminology).

52 Repeat steps 8, 9 and 10 using a third 1m (3¼ft) length of rope as the holding cord.

53 Repeat steps 2–7.

54 Continue the alternating double square knot pattern for two more rows.

55 Repeat steps 8, 9 and 10 using the remaining 1m (3¼ft) length of rope as the holding cord.

56 Trim the remaining cords to 35cm (13¾in).

57 Use the 2m (6½ft) length of rope to make a hanging cord by tying an overhand knot (see Overhand Knot) at each end of the dowel.

BASIC PLANT HANGER

What better way than a macramé plant hanger to show off some beautiful greenery in your kitchen or living areas? This simple pattern is the perfect place to start to learn the technique of making hanging homes for your houseplants. For a fresh take on this timeless classic, substitute your flowerpots with a favourite vase and fill it with some fresh hand-picked blooms.

MATERIALS:

- 43m (142ft) length of 5mm (¼in) rope
- 4.5cm (1¾in) metal ring
- 30cm (1ft) length of 2.5mm (⅛in) cotton twine

KNOTS AND TECHNIQUES:

- Wrapped Knot
- Square Knot
- Half Knot Spiral
- Overhand Knot
- Wrapping a Ring
- Mounting Techniques
- Fraying

PREPARATION:

- Cut eight 5m (16½ft) lengths of 5mm (¼in) rope
- Cut three 1m (3¼ft) lengths of 5mm (¼in) rope

Method

1 Wrap the 4.5cm (1¾in) metal ring with a 1m (3¼ft) length of rope (see Wrapping a Ring).

2 Mount the eight 5m (16½ft) lengths of rope onto the ring by folding them in half over the inside of the ring. (See Mounting Techniques for preparing to start.)

3 Using a 1m (3¼ft) length of rope, secure all of the cords together directly under the ring with a 4cm (1½in) wrapped knot (see Wrapped Knot).

4 Directly under the wrapped knot, separate the cords into four groups of four cords. Each group now becomes a sinnet (see Knotting Terminology). Repeat steps 5–8 for each sinnet.

5 Tie three square knots (see Square Knot).

6 Drop down 5cm (2in) and tie another three square knots.

7 Drop down 7cm (2¾in) and tie a half knot spiral with ten half knots (see Half Knot Spiral).

8 Drop down 7cm (2¾in) and tie three square knots.

9 Drop down 13cm (5⅛in). Alternate cords by bringing two cords together from each adjacent sinnet and tie one square knot.

10 Drop down 9cm (3½in). Alternate cords by bringing two cords together from each adjacent sinnet and tie one square knot.

11 Drop down 13cm (5⅛in). Bring all the cords together firmly and secure with an overhand knot (see Overhand Knot) using the 30cm (1ft) length of cotton twine.

12 Using the remaining 1m (3¼ft) length of rope, cover the cotton twine with a 4cm (1½in) wrapped knot.

13 Trim cords to 30cm (1ft) and fray (see Fraying).

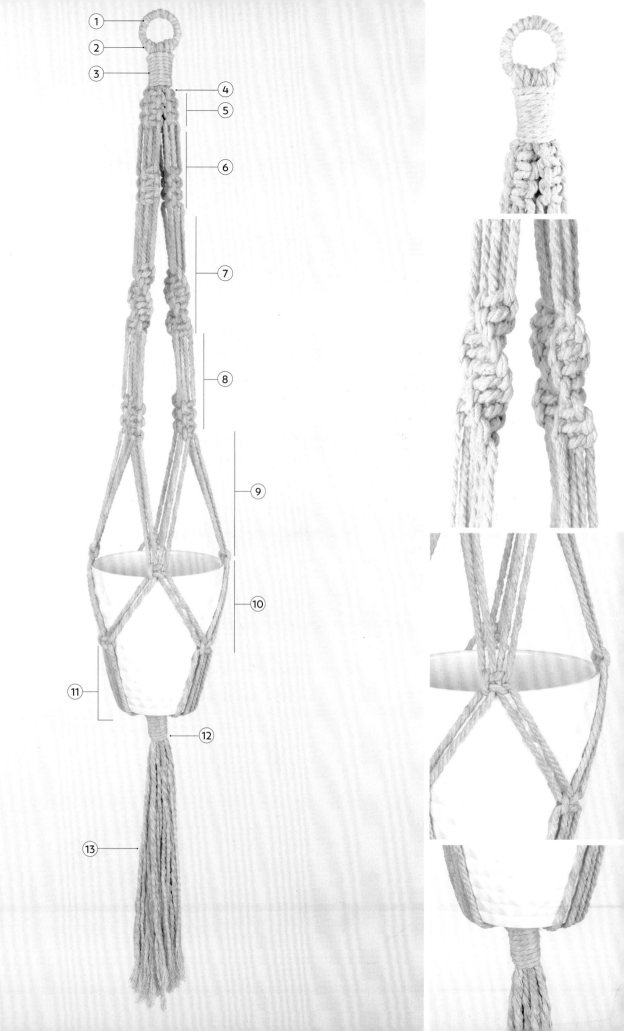

ADVANCED PLANT HANGER

MATERIALS:

- 393m (1,291ft) length of 4mm (5/32in) rope

- Metal rings: one 8cm (3⅛in); two 13cm (5⅛in); two 29cm (11⅜in)

KNOTS & TECHNIQUES:

- Wrapped Knot

- Chinese Crown Knot

- Double Half Hitch

- Square Knot

- Half Knot

- Reverse Lark's Head Knot

- Alternating Square Knot Pattern

- Overhand Knot

- Wrapping a Ring

- Mounting Techniques

This beautiful, large-scale plant hanger uses rings to create a basket-like enclosure for your favourite plant, but equally it stands – or should that be hangs? – alone as a super stylish home décor piece. We recommend you warm up to this more advanced plant hanger pattern by trying both the simple plant hanger and the hanging basket projects first.

PREPARATION:

- Cut fifty-six 3.5m (11½ft) lengths of 4mm (5/32in) rope

- Cut twenty-four 8m (26¼ft) lengths of 4mm (5/32in) rope

- Cut two 1m (3¼ft) lengths of 4mm (5/32in) rope

- Cut two 1.5m (5ft) lengths of 4mm (5/32in) rope

Method

1   Wrap the 8cm (3⅛in) metal ring with a 1m (3¼ft) length of rope (see Wrapping a Ring).

2   Mount the twenty-four 8m (26¼ft) lengths of rope onto the wrapped ring by folding them in half over the inside of the ring. (See Mounting Techniques for preparing to start.)

3   Using a 1.5m (5ft) length of rope, secure all of the cords together directly under the ring with a 4cm (1½in) wrapped knot (see Wrapped Knot).

4   Separate the cords into four groups of twelve cords and tie eight Chinese crown knots (see Chinese Crown Knot).

5   Drop down 10cm (4in) and place all the cords inside one of the 13cm (5⅛in) metal rings. The metal ring sitting horizontally is now to be used as the holding cord (see Knotting Terminology). Keeping the ring level, tie double half hitches (see Half Hitch Knots) with all cords onto the ring.

6   Secure the cord to the ring by tying a row of twelve square knots (see Square Knot) directly beneath the ring.

7   Alternate cords (see Knotting Terminology), drop down 3cm (1⅛in) and tie a row of twelve square knots.

8   Alternate cords, drop down 3cm (1⅛in) and tie another row of twelve square knots.

9   Place all cords inside the second 13cm (5⅛in) metal ring, which now becomes the holding cord. Keeping the ring horizontal and level, tie double half hitches with all cords onto the ring.

10 Separate the cords into four groups of twelve cords. Each group now becomes a sinnet (see Knotting Terminology). Repeat steps 11–17 for each sinnet.

11 Tie a row of three half knots (see Half Knot).

12 Directly beneath, alternate cords and tie a row of two half knots.

13 Directly beneath, alternate cords and tie a row of three half knots.

14 Continue this alternating half knot pattern for another five rows.

15 Directly beneath, tie a row of three square knots.

16 Drop down 25cm (10in) and tie a row of three square knots.

17 Repeat steps 11–15.

18 Place all cords inside one of the 29cm (11⅜in) metal rings. The metal ring sitting horizontally is now to be used as the holding cord. Keeping the ring level at all times and working on one sinnet at a time, tie double half hitches with all cords onto the ring, so that the sinnets are sitting on the ring in four separate groups equally spaced apart.

19 To cover the ring in between each of the secured sinnets, add fourteen 3.5m (11½ft) lengths of rope using reverse lark's head knot (see Reverse Lark's Head Knot) – a total of fifty-six lengths in all.

20 Directly beneath the ring, tie a row of twenty 8-cord square knots using four filler cords and two working cords on either side.

21 Drop down 1cm (⅜in), alternate cords and tie another row of twenty 8-cord square knots.

22 Continue the alternating square knot pattern (see Alternating Square Knot Pattern) for ten more rows with spaces of 1cm (⅜in) in between the rows.

23 Place all cords inside the second 29cm (11⅜in) metal ring. The metal ring sitting horizontally is now to be used as the holding cord. Keeping the ring level at all times, tie double half hitches with all cords onto the ring.

24 Gather the rope firmly and bring it upwards until it is centred and level with the second 29cm (11⅜in) metal ring. This will create a base for the plant hanger. Secure with a double overhand knot (see Overhand Knot) using the remaining 1m (3¼ft) length of rope.

25 Using the remaining 1.5m (5ft) length of rope, tie a 3.5cm (1⅜in) wrapped knot over the top of the double overhand knot.

26 Trim cords to the desired length.

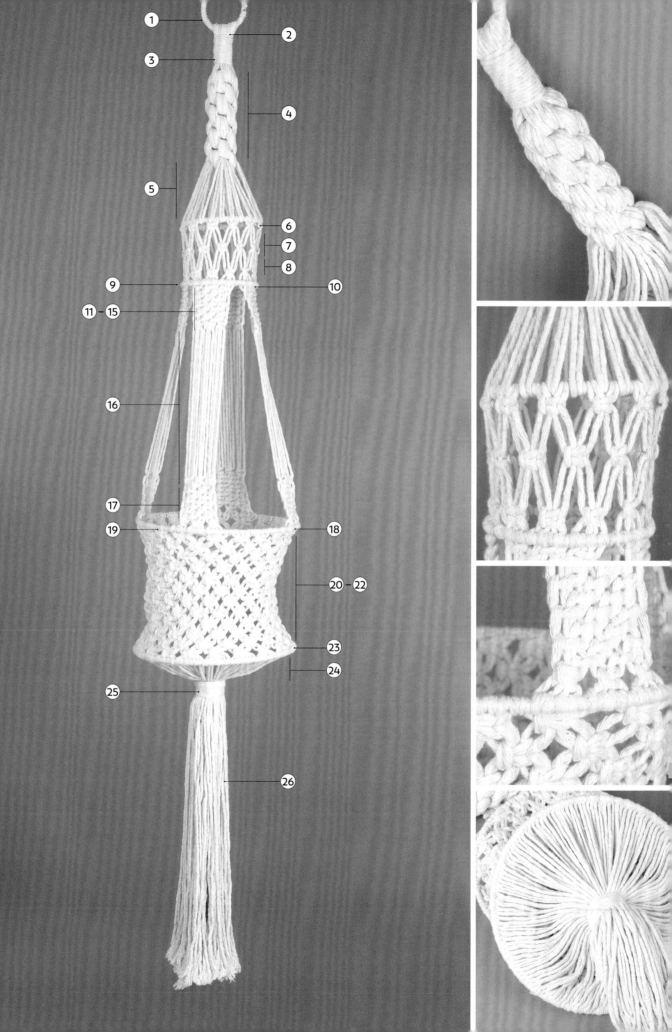

CUSHION DECORATION

Makeover a plain cushion cover with a beautiful macramé panel made from an alternating square knot pattern with a feature bead insertion. The completed panel is hand-sewn to your cushion top. Once you have mastered the first one, why not try making more in different sizes and shapes? We've chosen a natural calico cover to perfectly complement the natural cotton rope, and hand washing is recommended.

MATERIALS:

- 54.7m (182½ft) length of 5mm (¼in) rope

- Three wooden beads, 2.5cm (1in) long x 2cm (¾in) wide with a 1cm (⅜in) hole

- Hot glue gun

- 40 x 40cm (16 x 16in) cushion cover and insert

KNOTS & TECHNIQUES:

- Reverse Lark's Head Knot

- Square Knot

- Alternating Square Knot Pattern

- Half Hitch

- Overhand Knot

- Numbering Cords

PREPARATION:

- Cut eighteen 3m (10ft) lengths of 5mm (¼in) rope

- Cut two 35cm (13¾in) lengths of 5mm (¼in) rope

Method

1 Secure one of the 35cm (13¾in) lengths of rope to a project board with T-pins (or to a flat surface with adhesive tape), keeping it straight and firm. This becomes your holding cord (see Knotting Terminology).

2 Mount the eighteen 3m (10ft) lengths of rope onto the holding cord using reverse lark's head knots (see Reverse Lark's Head Knot), centring the rope lengths in the middle of the holding cord so that there is approximately 6–7cm (2⅜–2¾in) of uncovered holding cord at either end. The width of the mounted rope should be approximately 22cm (8⅝in).

3 Directly beneath the row of reverse lark's head knots, tie a row of nine square knots (see Square Knot).

4 Alternate cords (see Knotting Terminology) and tie a row of eight square knots.

5 Continue an alternating square knot pattern for a further seven rows (see Alternating Square Knot Pattern).

6 Number the cords 1 to 36 (see Numbering Cords). Directly beneath the last row of square knots, tie a square knot with cords 3–6 and another square knot with cords 7–10.

7 Thread a wooden bead onto cords 14 and 15, so that it sits directly against the square knot above it.

8 Thread a wooden bead onto cords 18 and 19, so that it sits directly against the square knot above it.

9 Thread a wooden bead onto cords 22 and 23, so that it sits directly against the square knot above it.

10 In line with the row, tie a square knot with cords 27–30 and another square knot with cords 31–34.

11 Renumber the cords 1 to 36. Creating a new row, tie square knots with cords 1–4, 5–8 and 9–12 and with cords 25– 28, 29–32 and 33–36. The bottom of the beads should now be in line with this row of square knots.

12 Alternate cords (see Knotting Terminology) and tie a row of eight square knots directly beneath.

13 Alternate cords and continue an alternating square knot pattern for seven more rows.

14 Take the remaining 35cm (13¾in) length of rope and place it over all the cords, so that the ends of the rope are even at each side. This is now to be used as the holding cord.

15 Tie all the cords onto the holding cord with half hitches (see Half Hitch Knots), and then trim them to 3cm (1⅛in).

16 Tie a tight overhand knot (see Overhand Knot) at each end of the holding cords, making sure the knot is pressing firmly against the sides of your work. Trim the holding cords to 4cm (1½in).

17 Turn the macramé panel over and use the hot glue gun to secure all the cord ends to the back of the design.

18 Turn the macramé panel to the right side and hand stitch it to the front of your cushion cover.

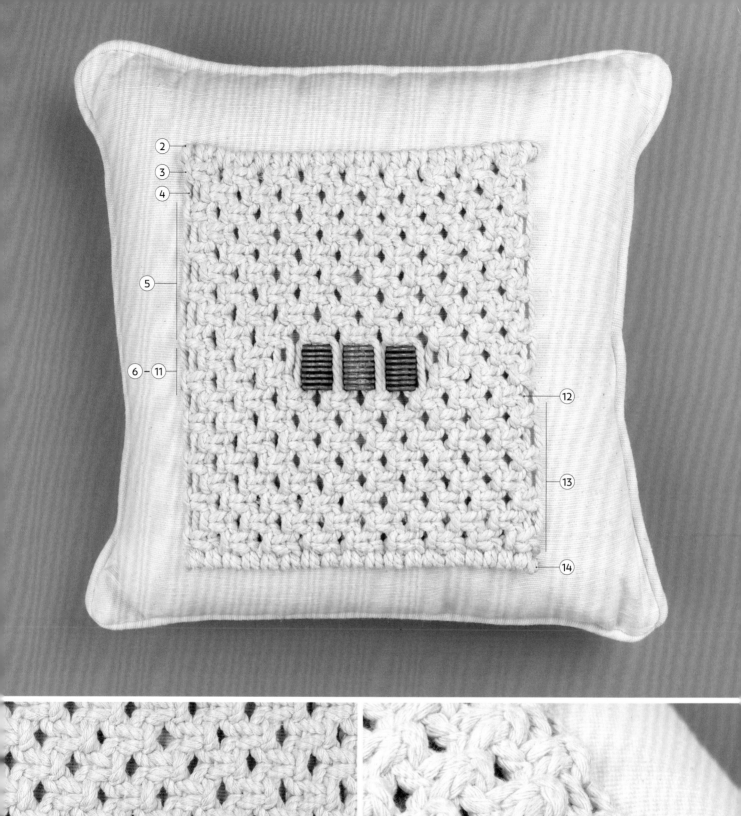

CIRCLE WALL HANGING

• • •

MATERIALS:

• 158.4m (527ft) length of 8mm (⁵⁄₁₆in) rope

• Metal rings: one 6cm (2⅜in); one 29cm (11⅜in); one 55cm (22in); one 65cm (25½in)

KNOTS & TECHNIQUES:

• Reverse Lark's Head Knot

• Square Knot

• Double Half Hitch

• Half Knot Spiral

• Fraying

This multifunctional, large-scale wall hanging can also be used as a small rug. Just a few basic knots are used to create the distinctive form of the piece and you can change the colour of the rope to suit your décor. If you intend to use the piece as a rug, jute makes a practical alternative to cotton rope.

PREPARATION:

• Cut forty-eight 3m (10ft) lengths of 8mm (⁵⁄₁₆in) rope

• Cut twenty-four 60cm (23½in) lengths of 8mm (⁵⁄₁₆in) rope

Method

1 Mount sixteen 3m (10ft) lengths of rope onto the 6cm (2⅜in) metal ring using reverse lark's head knots (see Reverse Lark's Head Knot), so that the mounted rope covers the ring. Place the ring on a flat surface so that the cords radiate out from the ring.

2 Directly beneath the ring, tie eight square knots (see Square Knot) around the diameter of the ring.

3 Alternate cords (see Knotting Terminology), drop down 4cm (1½in) and tie a row of eight square knots, keeping the ring flat on the work surface and the cords radiating out from the ring.

4 Tie another eight square knots directly beneath.

5 Place the 29cm (11⅜in) metal ring on top of the cords, ensuring it is evenly spaced from the first ring all the way around. This is now to be used as the holding cord.

6 Tie the cords onto the ring with double half hitches (see Half Hitch Knots), ensuring that each of the cord groups is evenly spaced around the ring.

7 To cover the ring in between the cord groups, mount four 3m (10ft) lengths of rope with reverse lark's head knots in each of the eight spaces, using all of the thirty-two remaining 3m (10ft) lengths.

8 Directly beneath the ring, tie twenty-four square knots around the diameter of the ring.

9 Take four adjacent cords beneath one of the square knots tied in step 8 and work six more square knots to create a sinnet (see Knotting Terminology) of seven square knots with no spaces in between.

10 Take the next four cords and create a half knot spiral sinnet made with twelve half knots (see Half Knot Spiral).

11 Repeat steps 9 and 10 to continue this pattern all the way around the ring, alternating square knot and half knot spiral sinnets.

12 Place the 55cm (22in) metal ring on top of the cords, ensuring it is evenly spaced from the second ring all the way around. This is now to be used as the holding cord. Tie the cords onto the ring with double half hitches and ensure the sinnets are evenly spaced around the ring.

13 Mount the twenty-four 60cm (23½in) lengths of rope onto the ring, one in each of the spaces between the sinnets, using reverse lark's head knots.

14 Directly beneath the ring, tie thirty-six square knots around the diameter of the ring.

15 Tie another thirty-six square knots directly beneath the previous row.

16 Place the 65cm (25½in) metal ring on top of the cords, ensuring it is evenly spaced from the third ring all the way around. This is now to be used as the holding cord. Tie the cords onto the ring with double half hitches.

17 Trim the cords to 6cm (2⅜in) and fray (see Fraying).

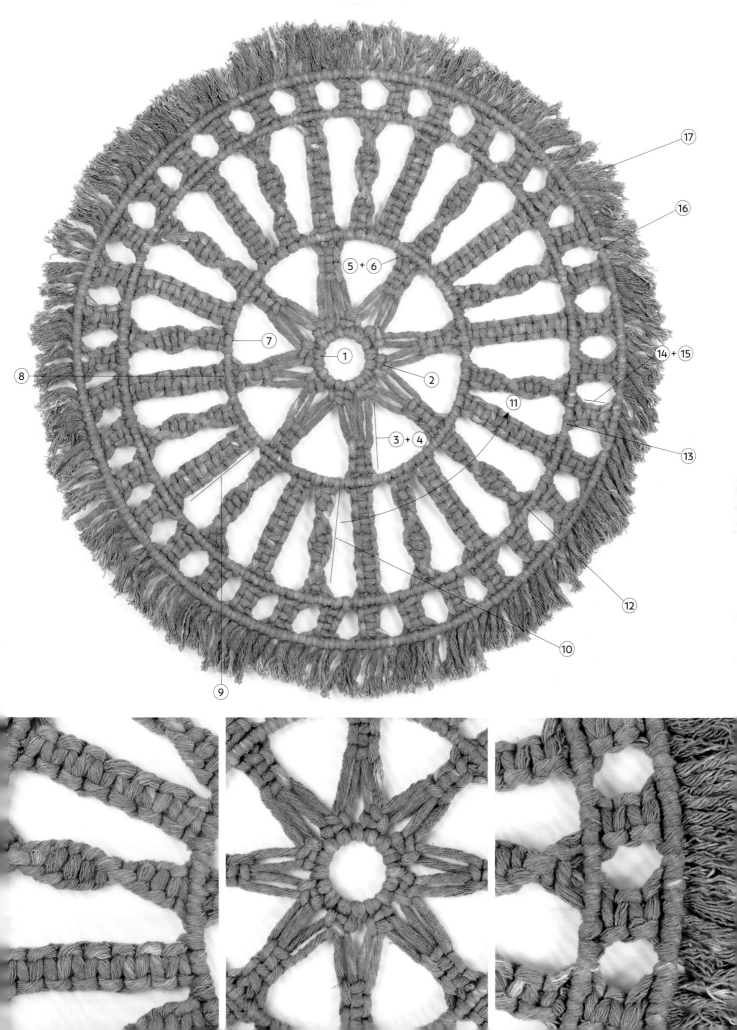

● ● ●

SIMPLE BUNTING

MATERIALS:

- 72.4m (237½ft) length of 5mm (¼in) rope

KNOTS & TECHNIQUES:

- Overhand Knot
- Reverse Lark's Head Knot
- Square Knot
- Decreasing Square Knot Pattern
- Diagonal Double Half Hitch
- Numbering Cords
- Fraying

Strings of bunting are such a sweet accessory and they can be used in so many ways, as a beautiful accent for nursery or a child's room, to decorate a baby shower, or simply to adorn the shelves, walls and windows of your home. This simple bunting has a length of eleven flags giving you plenty of opportunity to perfect the decreasing square knot pattern.

PREPARATION:

- Cut eighty-eight 80cm (31½in) lengths of 5mm (¼in) rope
- Cut one 2m (6½ft) length of 5mm (¼in) rope

Method

1 Tie an overhand knot (see Overhand Knot) at each end of the 2m (6½ft) length of rope to prevent it from fraying. This will become your holding cord (see Knotting Terminology). We have found that the best way to secure the holding cord ready to begin work is to tie it between the sides of a clothes rack/rail and to make sure that the holding cord is tight and straight. Alternatively, you could secure it to a flat surface such as a wall or a table using a strong adhesive tape.

2 You are now going to start tying your first flag at the centre of the holding cord: mount eight of the 80cm (31½in) lengths of rope onto the holding cord using reverse lark's head knots (see Reverse Lark's Head Knot). The width of the mounted rope should be 10cm (4in).

3 Tie a row of four square knots (see Square Knot) directly beneath the holding cord.

4 Continue to tie rows of square knots in a decreasing square knot pattern (see Decreasing Square Knot Pattern) to finish with a single square knot in the last row.

5 Number the cords 1 to 16 (see Numbering Cords). Make cord 1 a holding cord: bring it down diagonally left to right along the edge of the decreasing square knot pattern to the centre point and tie diagonal double half hitches (see Half Hitch Knots) with cords 2–8.

6 Make cord 16 a holding cord; bring it down diagonally right to left along the edge of the decreasing square knot pattern to the centre point and tie diagonal double half hitches with cords 9–15.

7 Tie cords 1 and 16 together with a double overhand knot (see Overhand Knot) to complete one flag.

8 Repeat steps 2–7 to make another ten flags, five to each side of the first (centre) flag, leaving a space of 4cm (1½in) on the holding cord in between each flag.

9 Trim the cords to the desired length and fray (see Fraying).

ADVANCED BUNTING

This bunting pattern gives you the opportunity to create a more intricate design of sweet little heart-shaped flags. In fact, each flag features a double heart-shape motif, with a small heart stacked on top of a larger one. Use different colour combinations for the flags to suit the occasion you are celebrating or to match your home décor.

MATERIALS:

- 28.4m (93½ft) length of 5mm (¼in) rope, natural

- 35.2m (116ft) length of 5mm (¼in) rope, in colours of your choice

KNOTS & TECHNIQUES:

- Overhand Knot

- Reverse Lark's Head Knot

- Square Knot

- Diagonal Double Half Hitch

- Numbering Cords

- Fraying

PREPARATION:

- Cut one 2m (6½ft) length of natural 5mm (¼in) rope

- Cut twenty-four 110cm (43½in) lengths of natural 5mm (¼in) rope

- Cut thirty-two 110cm (43½in) lengths of coloured rope

Method

1   Tie an overhand knot (see Overhand Knot) at each end of the 2m (6½ft) length of natural rope to prevent it from fraying. Mount the rope to a flat surface and secure. This now becomes your holding cord (see Knotting Terminology).

2   You are now going to start tying your first flag at the centre of the holding cord: mount eight of the 110cm (44½in) lengths of natural rope onto the holding cord using reverse lark's head knots (see Reverse Lark's Head Knot). The width of the mounted rope should be 10cm (4in).

3   Tie a row of four square knots directly beneath the holding cord.

4   Number the cords 1 to 16 (see Numbering Cords) and tie a square knot (see Square Knot) with cords 7–10.

5   Renumber cords 1 to 16. Make cord 5 a holding cord; bring it in a diagonal direction from left to right to sit just beneath the centre of the square knot tied in step 4 and tie diagonal double half hitches (see Half Hitch Knots) with cords 6–8.

6   Make cord 12 a holding cord: bring it in a diagonal direction from right to left to sit just beneath the centre of the square knot tied in step 4 and tie diagonal double half hitches (see Half Hitch Knots) with cords 11–9.

7   Cross over the holding cords (cords 5 and 12) so that they swap positions and renumber the cords 1 to 16.

8   Make cord 4 a holding cord: bring it in a diagonal direction left to right to sit just beneath the cross over point of the previous holding cords and tie diagonal double half hitches with cords 5–8.

9   Make cord 13 a holding cord: bring it in a diagonal direction right to left to sit just beneath the cross over point of the previous holding cords and tie diagonal double half hitches with cords 12–9.

10 Cross over the holding cords (cords 4 and 13) so that they swap positions and renumber the cords 1 to 16.

11 Make cord 3 a holding cord: bring it in a diagonal direction left to right as before and tie diagonal double half hitches with cords 4–8. To achieve a neat pointed flag shape, make sure that the first diagonal double half hitch you tie (cord 4) sits directly beneath the first diagonal double half hitch on the previous row.

12 Make cord 14 a holding cord: bring it in a diagonal direction right to left as before and tie diagonal double half hitches with cords 13–9.

13 Cross over the holding cords (cords 3 and 14) so that they swap positions and renumber the cords 1 to 16.

14 Make cord 2 a holding cord: bring it in a diagonal direction left to right as before and tie diagonal double half hitches with cords 3–8.

15 Make cord 15 a holding cord: bring it in a diagonal direction right to left as before and tie diagonal double half hitches with cords 14–9.

16 Cross over the holding cords (cords 2 and 15) so that they swap positions and renumber the cords 1 to 16.

17 Make cord 1 a holding cord: bring it in a diagonal direction left to right as before and tie diagonal double half hitches with cords 2–8.

18 Make cord 16 a holding cord: bring it in a diagonal direction right to left as before and tie diagonal double half hitches with cords 15–9.

19 Tie cords 1 and 16 together with a double overhand knot (see Overhand Knot) to complete one flag.

20 Repeat steps 2–19 to make another six flags, three to each side of the first flag, leaving a space of 6cm (2⅜in) in between each flag and finishing with a flag made with natural rope at each end of the bunting.

21 Trim the cords to the desired length and fray (see Fraying). We left the cords in the middle longer and cut the cords along the sides shorter to focus attention on the heart shape design.

• • •

INDOOR SWING

An uber-stylish indoor swing brings charm and character to your home, and functionally, it's a great way to add some extra seating. The natural cotton rope handles are made with half knot spirals that fork at the base to attach to a chunky wooden seat, an alluring contrast that makes this unusual piece of furniture perfectly suited to many home styles.

MATERIALS:

• 258m (846½ft) length of 5mm (¼in) rope

• Two 8cm (3⅛in) zinc-plated metal rings, heavy-duty (6mm/¼in)

• Two large zinc-plated carabiners

• One piece of pine wood measuring 48cm (19in) long x 18.5cm (7¼in) wide x 3cm (1⅛in) high

• Drill with 15mm (¹⁹⁄₃₂in) wood drill bit

• 180 grit (very fine) sandpaper

• Wood stain in your preferred colour

KNOTS & TECHNIQUES:

• Wrapped Knot

• Half Knot Spiral

• Overhand Knot

• Mounting Techniques

• Fraying

PREPARATION:

• Cut sixteen 16m (52½ft) lengths of 5mm (¼in) rope

• Cut two 1m (3¼ft) lengths of 5mm (¼in) rope

• At each corner of the wood, mark a hole position 2cm (¾in) from the sides, then drill the holes

• Lightly sand the wood to remove any rough or uneven surfaces, then stain to your desired colour

Method

1   Mount eight 16m (52½ft) lengths of rope onto one of the metal rings by folding them in half over the inside of the ring. (See Mounting Techniques for preparing to start.)

2   Tie a 4cm (1½in) wrapped knot (see Wrapped Knot) around all cords using one of the 1m (3¼ft) lengths of rope.

3   Separate the cords into three consecutive groups: group 1 – four cords; group 2 – eight cords; and group 3 – four cords.

4   Using group 1 and group 3 cords as the working cords and group 2 as the filler cords (see Knotting Terminology), tie a 16-cord half knot spiral with 103 half knots (see Half Knot Spiral).

5   Now separate the cords into two groups of eight cords.

6   Take the first group of eight cords and separate the cords into three consecutive groups: group 1 – two cords; group 2 – four cords; and group 3 – two cords.

7   Using group 1 and group 3 cords as the working cords and group 2 as the filler cords, tie an 8-cord half knot spiral with eighteen half knots (see Half Knot Spiral).

8   Repeat steps 6 and 7 for the second group of eight cords. The first of your swing handles is now complete.

9   Repeat steps 1–8 using the remaining eight 16m (52½ft) lengths of rope and the second metal ring to make a second swing handle, making sure that the half knot spiral designs on each of the swing handles are equal in length.

10 Place the pine wood seat horizontally and thread the cords of the half knot spirals through each of the drilled corner holes.

11 Turn the seat upside down and tie each group of cords with an overhand knot (see Overhand Knot) to secure the seat in place at each corner. Turn the seat the right way up and make sure it is sitting perfectly level.

12 Trim the cords to the desired length and fray (see Fraying).

13 Attach the carabiner hooks to the metal rings and the finished swing is ready to be hung up.

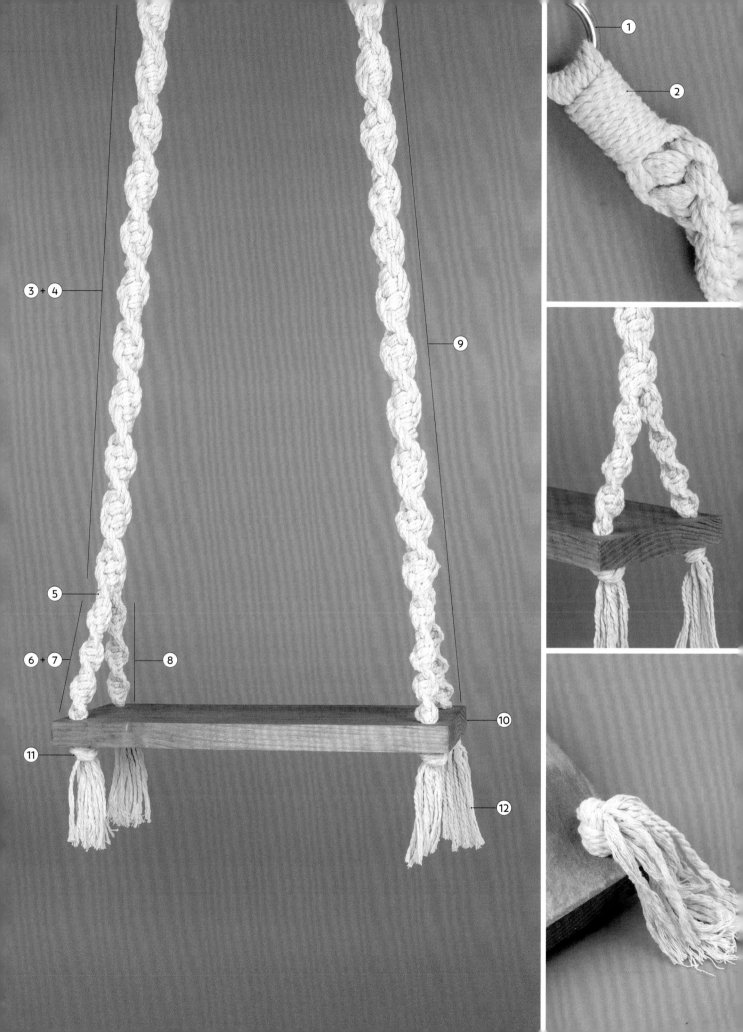

• • •

DECK CHAIR

Turn an everyday deck chair into a bespoke piece of furniture with this macramé design. Simply remove the fabric from the deck chair frame and follow the pattern to create your own masterpiece. If your deck chair differs in size from the one we have used, you may need to make alterations to the length and width of the macramé panel to fit, adjusting as necessary to make it the same dimensions as the original deck chair fabric.

MATERIALS:

• 304m (997½ft) length of 5mm (¼in) rope

• Deck chair frame 88cm (35¾in) high x 97cm (38⅛in) wide x 67cm (26⅜in) deep

• Hot glue gun

KNOTS & TECHNIQUES:

• Reverse Lark's Head Knot

• Square Knot

• Alternating Square Knot Pattern

• Double Half Hitch

• Overhand Knot

PREPARATION:

• Cut thirty-eight 8m (26¼ft) lengths of 5mm (¼in) rope

• Carefully remove the existing fabric from the deck chair frame

Method

1   Mount all thirty-eight 8m (26¼ft) lengths of rope to the top bar of the deck chair frame using reverse lark's head knots (see Reverse Lark's Head Knot), ensuring that the cords are evenly spaced apart. The width of the mounted rope should be approximately 47cm (18½in) (or the width of the original fabric).

2   Directly beneath, tie a row of nineteen square knots (see Square Knot) to secure the cords in place.

3   Directly beneath, alternate cords (see Knotting Terminology) and tie a row of eighteen square knots.

4   Continue an alternating square knot pattern for another three rows (see Alternating Square Knot Pattern) with no space between rows.

5   Alternate cords, drop down 3.5cm (1⅜in) and tie a row of eighteen square knots.

6   Alternate cords, drop down 3.5cm (1⅜in) and tie a row of nineteen square knots.

7   Directly beneath, tie a row of nineteen square knots.

8   Alternate cords and tie a row of eighteen square knots.

9   Directly beneath, tie a row of eighteen square knots.

10 Alternate cords and tie a row of nineteen square knots.

11 Directly beneath, tie a row of nineteen square knots.

12 Alternate cords, drop down 3.5cm (1⅜in) and tie a row of eighteen square knots.

13 Alternate cords, drop down 3.5cm (1⅜in) and tie a row of nineteen square knots.

14 Alternate cords, drop down 3.5cm (1⅜in) and tie a row of eighteen square knots.

15 Alternate cords, drop down 3.5cm (1⅜in) and tie a row of nineteen square knots.

16 Repeat steps 3–15.

17 Repeat steps 3–11.

18 Alternate cords, drop down 3cm (1⅛in) and tie a row of eighteen square knots.

19 Directly beneath, alternate cords and tie a row of nineteen square knots.

20 Now attach your macramé panel to the bottom bar of the deck chair: bring all cords underneath the bottom bar and secure each cord to the chair with a double half hitch knot (see Half Hitch Knots). Make sure your macramé panel has been pulled really tight before securing it to the bottom bar of the chair, so that it doesn't have too much give when it is being used.

21 Once all cords have been secured to the bottom bar, pull them as far as you can towards the underneath of the chair and tie them together in pairs – 1 and 2, 3 and 4, 5 and 6, 7 and 8, etc. – extremely tightly using double overhand knots (see Overhand Knot).

22 Trim the ends of the cords to approximately 5mm (¼in) long and glue them down flat using the hot glue gun.

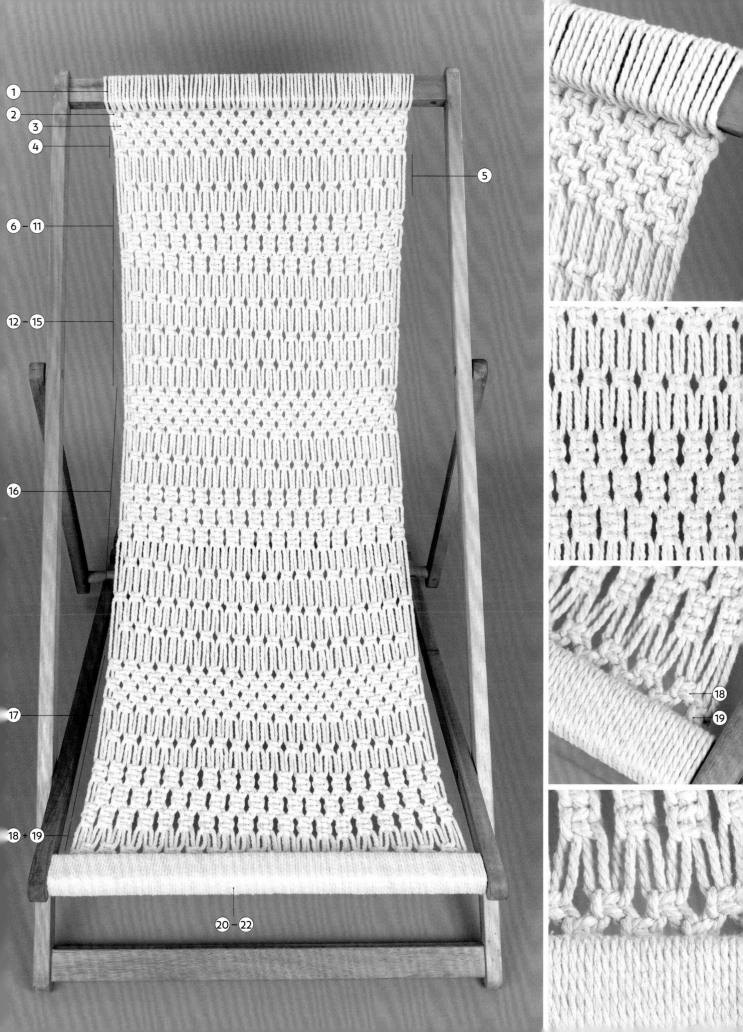

• • •

DOOR HANGING

This modern version of a classic, bead door curtain creates a breathtaking entranceway to any room and will make your home feel like a Bohemian palace. The pattern is made to fit a standard door frame, however you can easily alter the width or length of the macramé to fit your doorways.

MATERIALS:

• 368m (1,211ft) length of 5mm (¼in) rope

• 92cm (36¼in) length of 2.5cm (1in) dowel

• Six 30cm (1ft) lengths of twine

• Twelve wooden beads, 2cm (¾in) long x 2cm (¾in) wide with 1cm (⅜in) hole

KNOTS & TECHNIQUES:

• Reverse Lark's Head Knot

• Square Knot

• Decreasing Square Knot Pattern

• Diagonal Double Half Hitch

• Increasing Square Knot Pattern

• Alternating Square Knot Pattern

• Overhand Knot

• Wrapped Knot

• Mounting Techniques

• Numbering Cords

• Fraying

PREPARATION:

• Cut twenty-eight 8m (26¼ft) lengths of 5mm (¼in) rope

• Cut six 6m (19¾ft) lengths of 5mm (¼in) rope

• Cut twelve 5m (16½ft) lengths of 5mm (¼in) rope

• Cut fourteen 3m (10ft) lengths of 5mm (¼in) rope

• Cut six 1m (3¼ft) lengths of 5mm (¼in) rope

Method

1 Starting 4cm (1½in) from the left-hand end of the dowel, use reverse lark's head knots (see Reverse Lark's Head Knot) to mount all but the six 1m (3¼ft) lengths of the rope in the following order: fourteen 8m (26¼ft) lengths; three 6m (19¾ft) lengths; six 5m (16½ft) lengths; fourteen 3m (10ft) lengths; six 5m (16½ft) lengths; three 6m (19¾ft) lengths; fourteen 8m (26¼ft) lengths. The width of the mounted rope should be 84cm (33¼in) to leave 4cm (1½in) of uncovered dowel at the right-hand end; adjust the cords so evenly spaced. (See Mounting Techniques for preparing to start.)

2 Directly beneath the dowel, tie a row of thirty square knots (see Square Knot).

3 Working from left to right, number the cords 1 to 120 (see Numbering Cords) and separate into six groups as follows: group 1 – cords 1–12; group 2 – cords 13–36; group 3 – cords 37–60; group 4 – cords 61–84; group 5 – cords 85–108; group 6 – cords 109–120.

4 Starting at group 1 (cords 1–12), working left to right, leave out the first two cords and tie two square knots directly beneath the existing square knots.

5 For group 1 next row, working left to right, tie two square knots.

6 For group 1 next row, working left to right, leave out the first two cords and tie one square knot.

7 For group 1 next row, working left to right, tie one square knot.

8 For groups 2, 3, 4 and 5, working on each group one at a time, use six of the existing square knots to create a decreasing square knot pattern for each group (see Decreasing Square Knot Pattern) ending with a single square knot.

9 For group 6 (cords 109–120), working left to right, leave out the first two cords and tie two square knots directly beneath the existing square knots.

10 For group 6 next row, working left to right, leave out four cords and tie two square knots.

11 For group 6 next row, working left to right, leave out six cords and tie one square knot.

12 For group 6 next row, working left to right, leave out eight cords and tie one square knot.

13 Returning to group 1, make the furthermost cord on the right a holding cord: bring it down diagonally right to left to sit on top of the other eleven cords and along the edge of the diagonal square knot pattern; tie diagonal double half hitches with the remaining eleven cords in the group (see Half Hitch Knots).

14 For groups 2, 3, 4 and 5, working on each group one at a time, make the furthermost cord on the left a holding cord: bring it down diagonally left to right to sit on top of eleven cords and along the edge of the decreasing square knot pattern to the centre point, and tie diagonal double half hitches with the eleven cords. Now make the furthermost cord on the right a holding cord: bring it down diagonally right to left to sit on top of the remaining eleven cords in the group and along the edge of the decreasing square knot pattern to the centre point, and tie diagonal double half hitches with the eleven remaining cords.

15 For group 6, make the furthermost cord on the left a holding cord: bring it down diagonally left to right to sit on top of the other eleven cords and along the edge of the diagonal square knot pattern; tie diagonal double half hitches with the remaining eleven cords in the group.

16 Renumber the cords 1 to 120. Thread a single bead onto cords 24 and 25, cords 48 and 49, cords 72 and 73, and cords 96 and 97.

17 Tie a square knot with cords 11–14 in line with the row of beads.

18 Continue an increasing square knot pattern (see Increasing Square Knot Pattern) directly under the last tied square knot until you have a row of five square knots, then begin a decreasing square knot pattern (see Decreasing Square Knot Pattern) until you have worked a row with

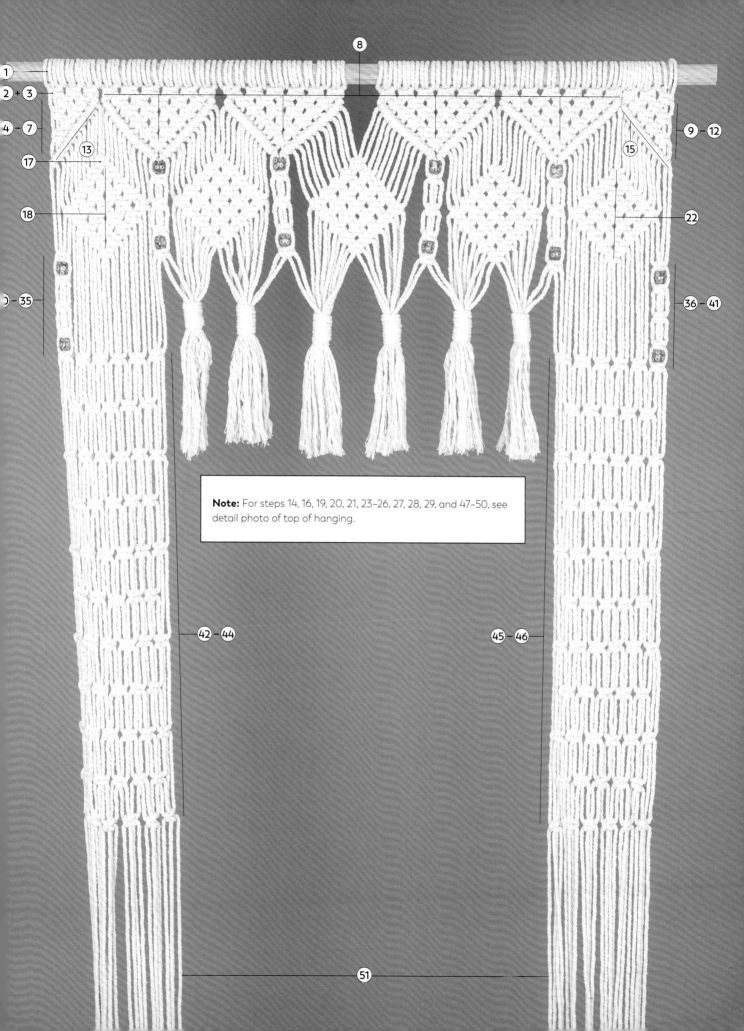

Note: For steps 14, 16, 19, 20, 21, 23–26, 27, 28, 29, and 47–50, see detail photo of top of hanging.

just one square knot to complete the diamond shape of the square knot pattern.

19 Tie a square knot with cords 35–38 in line with the row of beads and repeat step 18.

20 Tie a square knot with cords 59–62 in line with the row of beads and repeat step 18.

21 Tie a square knot with cords 83–86 in line with the row of beads and repeat step 18.

22 Tie a square knot with cords 107–110 in line with the row of beads and repeat step 18.

23 Underneath cords 24 and 25 where the first bead was placed, tie a square knot with cords 23–26.

24 Drop down 2.5cm (1in) and tie a square knot.

25 Drop down 2.5cm (1in) and tie a square knot.

26 Attach a single bead to the filler cords (see Knotting Terminology) of the previously tied square knot and secure the bead by tying a square knot directly beneath it.

27 Underneath cords 48 and 49 where the second bead was placed, tie a square knot with cords 47–50. Repeat steps 24–26.

28 Underneath cords 72 and 73 where the third bead was placed, tie a square knot with cords 71–74. Repeat steps 24–26.

29 Underneath cords 96 and 97 where the fourth bead was placed, tie a square knot with cords 95–98. Repeat steps 24–26.

30 Take cords 1–4 and tie a square knot in line with the last square knot at the bottom of the diamond shape.

31 Attach a single bead to the filler cords directly below the previously tied square knot.

32 Tie a square knot directly beneath the bead with cords 1–4.

33 Drop down 2.5cm (1in) and tie a square knot.

34 Drop down 2.5cm (1in) and tie a square knot.

35 Repeat steps 31 and 32.

36 Take cords 117–120 and tie a square knot in line with the last square knot at the bottom of the diamond shape.

37 Attach a single bead to the filler cords directly below the previously tied square knot.

38 Tie a square knot directly beneath the bead with cords 117–120.

39 Repeat steps 33 and 34.

40 Attach a single bead to the filler cords directly below the previously tied square knot.

41 Tie a square knot directly beneath the bead with cords 117–120.

42 Take cords 5–8 and tie a square knot in line with the last square knot tied with cords 1–4. Use cords 9–12, 13–16, 17–20, 21–24 to tie square knots in a row.

43 Alternate cords (see Knotting Terminology), drop down 5cm (2in) and tie a row of five square knots.

44 Continue an alternating square knot pattern (see Alternating Square Knot Pattern) for another nine rows leaving 5cm (2in) in between each row.

45 Take cords 113–116 and tie a square knot in line with the last square knot tied with cords 117–120. Use cords 109–112, 105–108, 101–104, 97–100 to tie square knots in a row.

46 Repeat steps 43 and 44. You now have the two long (outer) sides of the door hanging design.

47 To complete the top border of the door hanging, begin by grouping the middle cords into six groups of twelve cords: group 1 – cords 25–36; group 2 – cords 37–48; group 3 – cords 49–60; group 4 – cords 61–72; group 5 – cords 73–84; group 6 – cords 85–96.

48 Measuring approximately 31cm (12¼in) from the bottom of the dowel or about 7cm (2¾in) beneath the base of the diamond designs, use a 30cm (1ft) length of twine to firmly secure each group of cords with a double overhand knot (see Overhand Knot).

49 Use the remaining six 1m (3¼ft) lengths of rope to tie 4cm (1½in) wrapped knots (see Wrapped Knot) over the top of the double overhand knots.

50 Trim the ends of the rope below the wrapped knots to 15cm (6in) and fray (see Fraying).

51 Trim the ends of the rope on the long (outer) sides to 2m (6½ft) below the dowel.

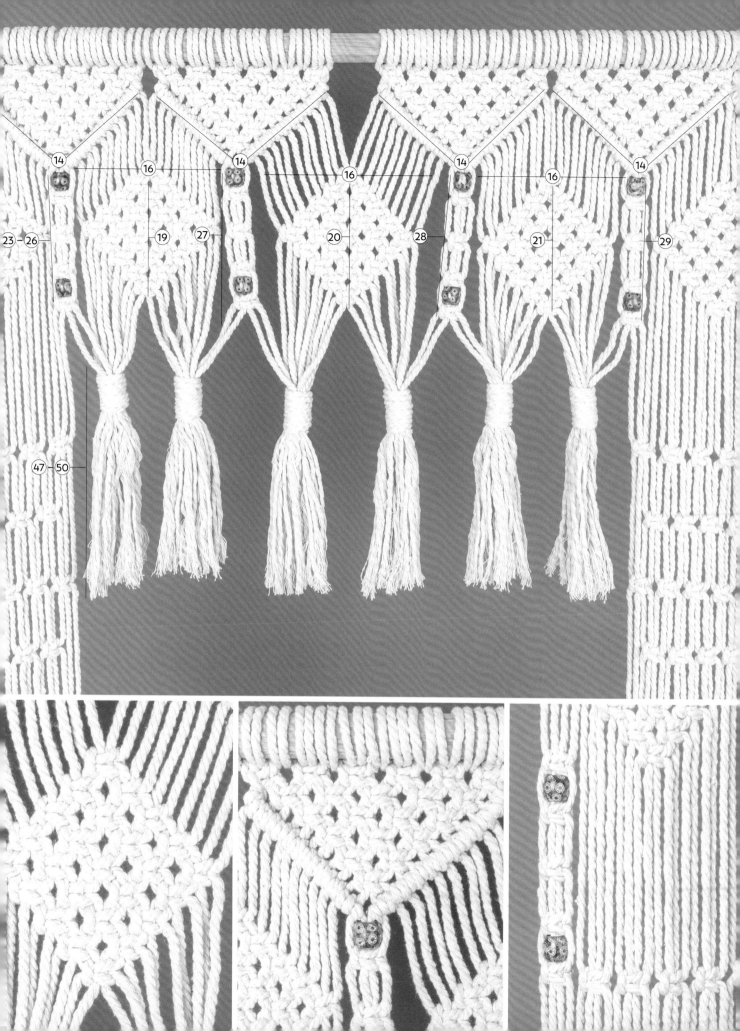

CELEBRATION ARCH

A larger scale version of a door hanging, the celebration arch creates an elegant special event backdrop that could be used either suspended from a wooden arbour or from a wall. Perfect for weddings, simply add floral bouquets to create a luxurious focal point. Alternatively, you could display it as a grand wall hanging in your home.

MATERIALS:

- 392m (1,300ft) length of 8mm (5⁄16in) rope

- 1.8m (6ft) length of 1.9cm (¾in) dowel

KNOTS & TECHNIQUES:

- Reverse Lark's Head Knot

- Square Knot

- Increasing Square Knot Pattern

- Decreasing Square Knot Pattern

- Alternating Square Knot Pattern

- Double Half Hitch

- Diagonal Double Half Hitch

- Mounting Techniques

- Numbering Cords

- Fraying

PREPARATION:

- Cut sixteen 7m (23ft) lengths of 8mm (5⁄16in) rope

- Cut sixteen 6m (19¾ft) lengths of 8mm (5⁄16in) rope

- Cut sixteen 4m (13¼ft) lengths of 8mm (5⁄16in) rope

- Cut twenty-four 3m (10ft) lengths of 8mm (5⁄16in) rope

- Cut twenty-four 2m (6½ft) lengths of 8mm (5⁄16in) rope

Method

1 Starting 8cm (3⅛in) from the left-hand end of the dowel and working from left to right, use reverse lark's head knots (see Reverse Lark's Head Knot) to mount the rope onto the dowel in the following order: eight 7m (23ft) lengths; eight 6m (19¾ft) lengths; eight 4m (13¼ft) lengths; twelve 3m (10ft) lengths; twenty-four 2m (6½ft) lengths; twelve 3m (10ft) lengths; eight 4m (13¼ft) lengths; eight 6m (19¾ft) lengths; eight 7m (23ft) lengths. Making sure to leave 8cm (3⅛in) of the dowel uncovered at the right-hand end, adjust the cords so that they are evenly spaced apart. (See Mounting Techniques for preparing to start.)

2 Directly beneath the dowel, tie a row of twenty-four 8-cord square knots (see Square Knot) using four filler cords and two working cords on either side (see Knotting Terminology).

3 Number the cords 1 to 192 (see Numbering Cords).

4 Drop down 6cm (2⅜in) and tie a square knot with cords 95–98.

5 Beginning with the square knot made with cords 95–98, work an increasing square knot pattern (see Increasing Square Knot Pattern) with rows tied directly beneath one another, finishing when you have a completed a row of nine square knots.

6 Directly beneath the row of nine square knots, begin a decreasing square knot pattern (see Decreasing Square Knot Pattern) until you have worked a row with just one square knot to complete a diamond shape pattern.

7 You have two groups of cords not used to create the diamond shape pattern: group 1 – cords 1–78; and group 2 – cords 115–192. For group 1, drop down 1.5cm (⅝in) and working left to right, alternate cords and tie a row of nine 8-cord square knots.

8 Continuing with group 1, drop down 1.5cm (⅝in) and working left to right, alternate cords and tie a row of nine 8-cord square knots.

9 Continuing with group 1, drop down 1.5cm (⅝in) and working left to right, alternate cords and tie a row of eight 8-cord square knots.

10 For group 2, drop down 1.5cm (⅝in) and working right to left, alternate cords and tie a row of nine 8-cord square knots.

11 Continuing with group 2, drop down 1.5cm (⅝in) and working right to left, alternate cords and tie a row of nine 8-cord square knots.

12 Continuing with group 2, drop down 1.5cm (⅝in) and working right to left, alternate cords and tie a row of eight 8-cord square knots.

13 For groups 1 and 2, continue this alternating (8-cord) square knot pattern (see Alternating Square Knot Pattern) with spaces of 1.5cm (⅝in) between each row for nine more rows, and for each consecutive row, leave out four cords towards the middle of the design. This will ensure that the pattern decreases from the middle outwards to begin to create an arched effect while remaining as a standard alternating pattern on the outer sides. You will now be left with a row of four 8-cord square knots on both groups 1 and 2.

14 For groups 1 and 2, alternate cords (see Knotting Terminology), drop down 1.5cm (⅝in) and tie a row of three 8-cord square knots.

15 For groups 1 and 2, alternate cords, drop down 1.5cm (⅝in) and tie a row of four 8-cord square knots.

16 For groups 1 and 2, continue this alternating (8-cord) square knot pattern with spaces of 1.5cm (⅝in) between each row for ten more rows. You will now begin to see the basic shape of the arbour.

17 Putting the outer panels to the side (thirty-two cords at each side), number the cords in the centre section of the design 1 to 128.

18 Make cord 47 a holding cord: bring it down diagonally right to left and tie a double half hitch (see Half Hitch Knots) to secure it to the space between the tenth and eleventh row of 8-cord square knots.

19 Tie cords 9–46 to the holding cord 47 with diagonal double half hitches (see Half Hitch Knots).

20 Make cord 82 a holding cord: bring it down diagonally left to right and tie a double half hitch to secure it to the space between the tenth and eleventh row of 8-cord square knots.

21 Tie cords 83–120 to the holding cord 82 with diagonal double half hitches.

22 Trim the cords of the outer panels (thirty-two cords at each side) to 2.4m (7¾ft).

23 Trim the cords in the centre section to your desired length in an arch shape and fray (see Fraying).

• • •

SHOPPING BAG

You can create this bright, bold shopping bag using a few simple knots. It is the perfect accessory to take with you on a trip to the market or when you are out and about running errands. You can be creative with your choice of handles to style your own unique carrier, but remember that the bag handles you choose must be able to fit the allocated cords.

MATERIALS:

• Three 32m (106ft) lengths of 5mm (¼in) rope in colours of your choice

• 60cm (23½in) length of 5mm (¼in) rope in a colour of your choice

• Two wooden bag handles of your choice with a minimum inner width of 12.5cm (4⅞in)

KNOTS & TECHNIQUES:

• Reverse Lark's Head Knot

• Square Knot

• Alternating Square Knot Pattern

• Double Half Hitch

• Overhand Knot

• Numbering Cords

• Fraying

PREPARATION:

• Cut eight 4m (13¼ft) lengths from each of the different coloured 32m lengths of 5mm (¼in) rope to give you twenty-four 4m (13¼ft) lengths in total

Method

1   Take your first bag handle and mount twelve 4m (13¼ft) lengths of rope onto it using reverse lark's head knot (see Reverse Lark's Head Knot), alternating the colours as you go. The width of the mounted rope should be 12.5cm (4⅞in). This will be handle number 1.

2   Take your second bag handle and mount the remaining twelve 4m (13¼ft) lengths of rope as described in step 1. This will be handle number 2.

3   Working first on handle 1, tie a row of six square knots (see Square Knot) really tightly directly beneath the handle.

4   Alternate cords (see Knotting Terminology), drop down 1.5cm (⅝in) and tie a row of five square knots.

5   Alternate cords, drop down 2cm (¾in) and tie a row of six square knots.

6   Continue with an alternating square knot pattern for two more rows with 2cm (¾in) spaces in between (see Alternating Square Knot Pattern).

7   Repeat steps 3–6 on handle 2 making sure that the knotted area on both handles 1 and 2 is equal in length.

8   For handle 1, number the cords 1 to 24 (see Numbering Cords).

9   For handle 2, number the cords 25 to 48.

10   Bring both handles together, so that the front of the design is facing outwards on both sides of the bag. To begin to join the sides of the bag, bring together cords 1 and 2 with 47 and 48 to tie a square knot 4cm (1½in) down, using cords 48 and 1 as the filler cords and cords 47 and 2 as the working cords (see Knotting Terminology).

11   Also 4cm (1½in) down, bring together cords 23 and 24 with 25 and 26 to tie a square knot, using cords 24 and 25 as the filler cords and 23 and 26 as the working cords.

12   In line with the two square knots tied in steps 10 and 11, continue to tie five more square knots on each side of the bag to create a row of twelve square knots around the bag.

13   Continue with an alternating square knot pattern around the bag with spaces of 4cm (1½in) between each row for another five rows.

14   Now join the bag together at the bottom edge. Lay the bag flat and align the handles evenly and make sure that on the bottom row the twelve square knots are sitting in a line, side by side, starting with a square knot from the back of the bag, then a square knot from the front of the bag, and alternating back and front square knots along the row.

15   Take the 60cm (23½in) length of rope and place it horizontally directly beneath the row of twelve square knots. This becomes your holding cord.

16   Working left to right, tie each cord onto the holding cord with a double half hitch knot (see Half Hitch Knots), making sure that all cords remain in the sequence created in step 14.

17   Push all cords tightly together over the holding cord, then tie a tight overhand knot (see Overhand Knot) at each end of the holding cord and let the ends of the holding cord hang down with the working cords.

18   Trim all cords to 5cm (2in) and fray if desired (see Fraying).

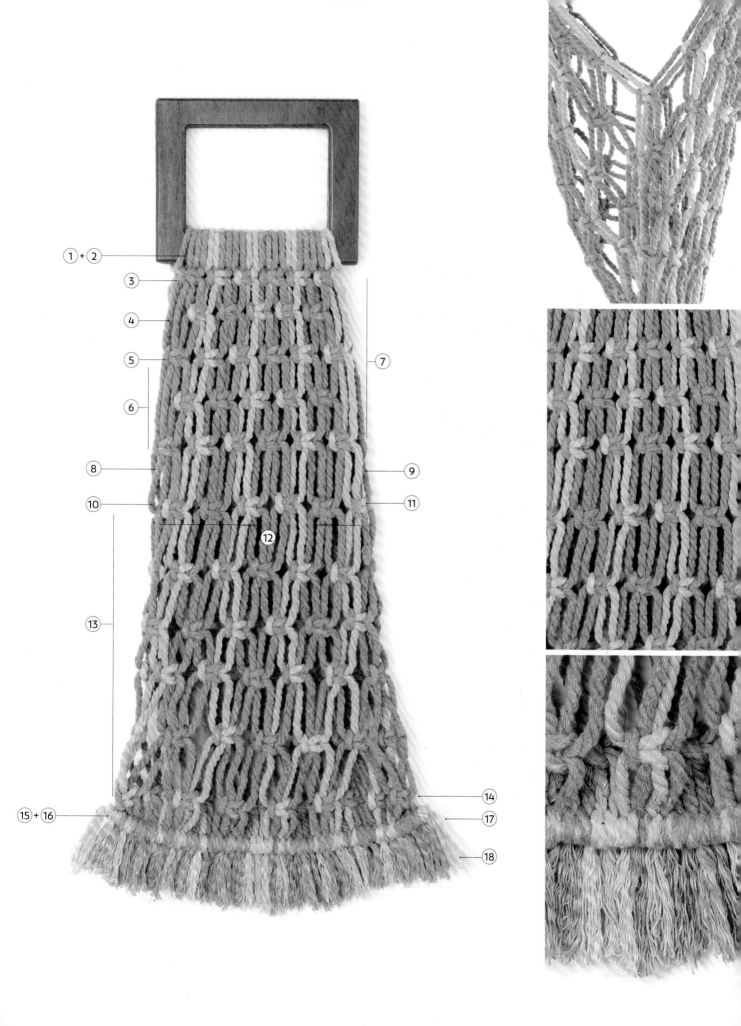

CLUTCH PURSE

A handmade macramé clutch purse is a sure-fire way to impress your friends on a night out on the town, and it's just the right size to carry your party essentials. With its pretty chevron flap and magnetic button closure, it is a must-have fashion accessory.

MATERIALS:

- 54m (180ft) length of 3mm (⅛in) jute
- 56m (186½ft) length of 3mm (⅛in) rope
- Hot glue gun
- Three 18mm (1¹⁄₁₆in) magnetic snap fasteners

KNOTS & TECHNIQUES:

- Reverse Lark's Head Knot
- Square Knot
- Alternating Square Knot Pattern
- Decreasing Square Knot Pattern
- Diagonal Double Half Hitch
- Overhand Knot
- Numbering Cords
- Weaving Finish
- Lacing Up

PREPARATION:

- Cut eighteen 3m (10ft) lengths of 3mm (⅛in) jute
- Cut eighteen 3m (10ft) lengths of 3mm (⅛in) rope
- Cut one 2m (6½ft) length of 3mm (⅛in) rope

Method

1 Secure the 2m (6½ft) length of rope to a project board with T-pins (see Tools & Materials), making sure it is straight and firm. This becomes your holding cord (see Knotting Terminology).

2 Alternating lengths of jute with lengths of rope, mount the eighteen 3m (10ft) lengths of jute and the eighteen 3m (10ft) lengths of rope onto the holding cord using reverse lark's head knots (see Reverse Lark's Head Knot). The width of the mounted cords should be 24.5cm (9¾in) and they should be centred on the holding cord.

3 Directly beneath the holding cord, tie a row of eighteen square knots (see Square Knot).

4 Aternate cords (see Knotting Terminology) and tie a row of seventeen square knots.

5 Continue an alternating square knot pattern (see Alternating Square Knot Pattern) with no spaces in between the rows for another forty-five rows, ending with a row of eighteen square knots. The total length of the macramé should be 27cm (10⅝in); if necessary, work more rows of square knots to bring the macramé to the required length, but remember it is important to end with a row of eighteen square knots.

6 Divide the cords into three groups of twenty-four cords: group 1 – cords 1–24; group 2 – cords 25–48; and group 3 – cords 49–72. Complete steps 7– 15 on each of the three groups of cords to create what will be the front flap chevron edge on the finished bag.

7 On each of the three groups of cords, work a decreasing square knot pattern (see Decreasing Square Knot Pattern) directly beneath the last row tied, beginning with six square knots and finishing with one square knot in the last row.

8 Number the cords in each of the three groups 1 to 24 (see Numbering Cords).

9 Make cord 1 a holding cord; bring it down diagonally left to right along the edge of the pattern to sit directly beneath the single square knot and tie diagonal double half hitches with cords 2–12 (see Half Hitch Knots).

10 Make cord 24 a holding cord; bring it down diagonally right to left along the edge of the pattern to sit directly beneath the single square knot and tie diagonal double half hitches with cords 13–23.

11 Cross over the holding cords (cords 1 and 24) so that they swap positions.

12 Now renumber the cords in each group 1 to 24.

13 Make cord 1 a holding cord; bring it down left to right so it sits directly beneath the row of diagonal double half hitches, and tie diagonal double half hitches with cords 2–12.

14 Make cord 24 a holding cord; bring it down right to left so it sits directly beneath the row of diagonal double half hitches, and tie diagonal double half hitches with cords 13–23.

15 Tie holding cords 1 and 24 together with a double overhand knot (see Overhand Knot).

16 Remove the macramé from the project board. Flip the macramé over and use the weaving finish technique (see Weaving Finish) to conceal the cords along the chevron edge. (Do not trim the holding cord along the straight edge.)

17 Trim the cords in each group to 5mm (¼in) and use a hot glue gun to secure them down.

18 To make your macramé into a clutch bag, keep the macramé wrong side facing up but orientate it so that the chevrons are at the top and the straight edge is at the bottom. Fold the bottom edge up by 12cm (4¾in) to make the pocket of the bag.

19 Use the holding cord to lace up the sides of the bag pocket (see Lacing Up), finishing with the cord on the inside of the purse, and secure with a double overhand knot.

20 Attach the magnetic snap fasteners to complete the purse. Use a hot glue gun to secure one part of each to the back side of the chevrons and the matching part to the front of the bag pocket, so that they match up when the flap is closed.

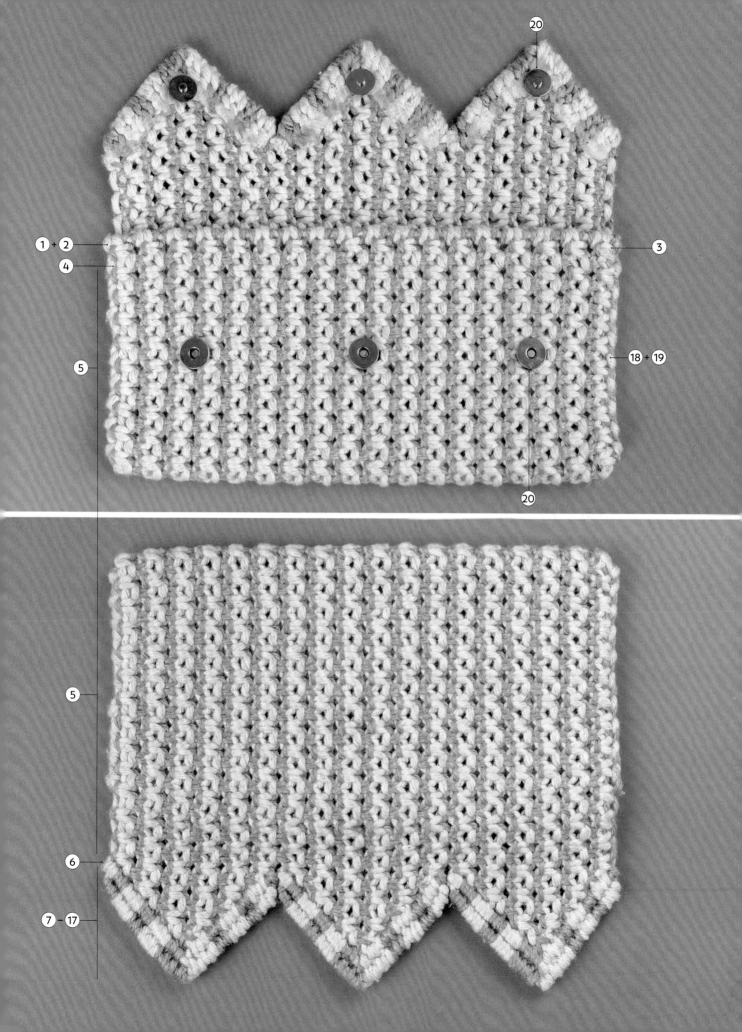

• • •

HANGING LIGHT

Made with a simple yet effective half knot spiral pattern, this hanging light is a great macramé starter project – it's an easy DIY undertaking that enables you to create something special for your home. To create something really awe inspiring, you could make multiple lights and hang them in conjunction with each other for your very own installation piece.

MATERIALS:

- 27m (89ft) length of 8mm (5⁄16in) rope
- 90cm (3ft) length of 4mm (5⁄32in) twisted rope
- 3m (10ft) DIY fabric cord set with plug, lead and E27 lamp holder

KNOTS & TECHNIQUES:

- Half Knot Spiral
- Wrapped Knot

PREPARATION:

- Firmly secure the lamp holder to a horizontal rail around 2m (6½ft) high so that the electrical cord hangs down vertically

Method

1   Fold the 27m (89ft) length of 8mm (5/16in) rope in half and place the halfway point behind the electrical cord and as close to the lamp holder as possible.

2   Begin to tie a half knot spiral (see Half Knot Spiral) using the electrical cord as the filler cord and the rope as the working cords, making sure to push your first half knot firmly against the lamp holder.

3   Continue to tie a half knot spiral until you are 3cm (1⅛in) from the plug.

4   Trim the excess rope just above the plug and push the ends down flat against the electrical cord.

5   Using the 90cm (3ft) length of 4mm (5/32in) twisted rope, tie a wrapped knot (see Wrapped Knot) starting directly under your last half knot and over the rope ends to finish directly above the plug so that all the electrical cord is covered.

①+②

③

④+⑤

③

• • •

PENDANT LANTERN

MATERIALS:

- 106m (351ft) length of 5mm (¼in) rope

- 2.5cm (1in) metal ring

- Cane rings: one 10cm (4in); one 13cm (5in); two 20cm (8in)

KNOTS & TECHNIQUES:

- Double Half Hitch

- Reverse Lark's Head Knot

- Square Knot

- Triple Half Hitch

The shape of this beautiful decoration has been inspired by the open latticework of Moroccan lanterns and it will provide you with a beautiful feature anywhere in your home. It could be styled as a mobile in a baby's nursery or to hang as a decorative piece alongside your hanging planters.

PREPARATION:

- Cut twenty-four 4m (13¼ft) lengths of 5mm (¼in) rope

- Cut two 5m (16½ft) lengths of 5mm (¼in) rope

Method

1 Take both of the 5m (16½ft) lengths of rope and fold them in half over the inside of the metal ring to give you four equal lengths of rope hanging down.

2 Place all four cords inside the 10cm (4in) cane ring. The cane ring sitting horizontally is now to be used as the holding cord (see Knotting Terminology).

3 Take two adjacent cords, drop down 30cm (12in) and tie the cords onto the ring with double half hitches (see Half Hitch Knots). Repeat to tie the remaining two cords onto the opposite side of the cane ring.

4 Attach twenty-four of the 4m (13¼ft) lengths of rope to the cane ring – twelve cords to each half – using reverse lark's head knot (see Reverse Lark's Head Knot).

5 Secure the cords to the ring by tying a row of thirteen square knots (see Square Knot) directly beneath the cane ring.

6 Alternate cords (see Knotting Terminology), drop down 7cm (2¾in) and tie a row of thirteen square knots.

7 Alternate cords, drop down 7cm (2¾in) and tie another row of thirteen square knots.

8 Place all cords inside one of the 20cm (8in) cane rings. This cane ring sitting horizontally is now to be used as the holding cord. Tie all cords onto the cane ring using triple half hitches (see Half Hitch Knots).

9 Secure the cords to the cane ring by tying a row of thirteen square knots directly beneath.

10 Alternate cords, drop down 3cm (1⅛in) and tie a row of thirteen square knots.

11 Alternate cords, drop down 3cm (1⅛in) and tie another row of thirteen square knots.

12 Repeat steps 8 and 9 with the second 20cm (8in) cane ring.

13 Alternate cords, drop down 4.5cm (1¾in) and tie a row of thirteen square knots.

14 Alternate cords, drop down 4.5cm (1¾in) and tie another row of thirteen square knots.

15 Place all cords inside the 13cm (5in) cane ring. This cane ring sitting horizontally is now to be used as the holding cord. Tie all cords onto the cane ring using double half hitches.

16 Trim the cords to 65cm (25½in) or to your desired length.

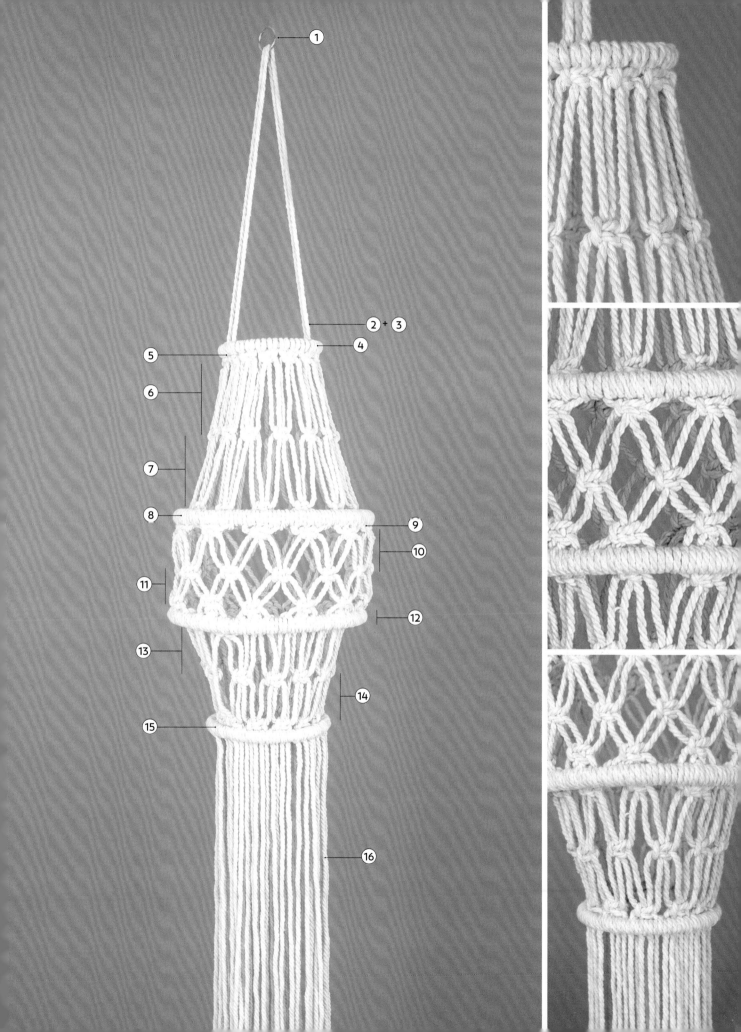

HOOP EARRINGS

MATERIALS:

- 2.6m (9ft) length of 1mm (1/32in) nylon bead cord in a colour of your choice

- Pair of 4cm (1½in) hoop earrings

- Six 4mm (5/32in) round metallic beads with a 2mm (3/32in) hole

KNOTS & TECHNIQUES:

- Square Knot

- Overhand Knot

If you fancy trying your hand at the art of macramé jewellery, this project is a great place to begin. A pair of shop-bought hoop earrings are covered with an easy square knot pattern, embellished with round metallic beads. They are so simple-to-make that you'll want to create several pairs in a variety of colours to complement your fashion choices.

PREPARATION:

- Cut two 1.3m (4½ft) lengths of 1mm (1/32in) nylon bead cord

Method

1. Fold one of the 1.3m (4½ft) lengths of nylon bead cord in half over the inside of one of the hoop earrings.

2. Secure the hoop earring to a project board using T-pins (see Tools & Materials). The hoop will be used as your filler cord and each side of the folded cord as your working cords (see Knotting Terminology).

3. Tie a firm square knot (see Square Knot) as close as possible to where the connector inserts into the hoop.

4. Tie a sinnet (see Knotting Terminology) of fifteen square knots working your way around the hoop (your filler cord). Push the knots firmly together once the sinnet is complete.

5. Thread a metal bead onto the earring hoop and push it firmly against the square knot sinnet.

6. Directly beneath the bead, tie a sinnet of three square knots.

7. Repeat step 5.

8. Repeat step 6.

9. Repeat step 5.

10. Directly beneath the bead, tie a sinnet of sixteen square knots to finish just before the connector.

11. Tie a tight double overhand knot with both cords (see Overhand Knot).

12. Trim the cords and carefully singe the ends to prevent fraying. Use a flame to melt the cord ends but be sure to stop before they char.

13. Repeat steps 1–12 with the second hoop earring to complete the pair.

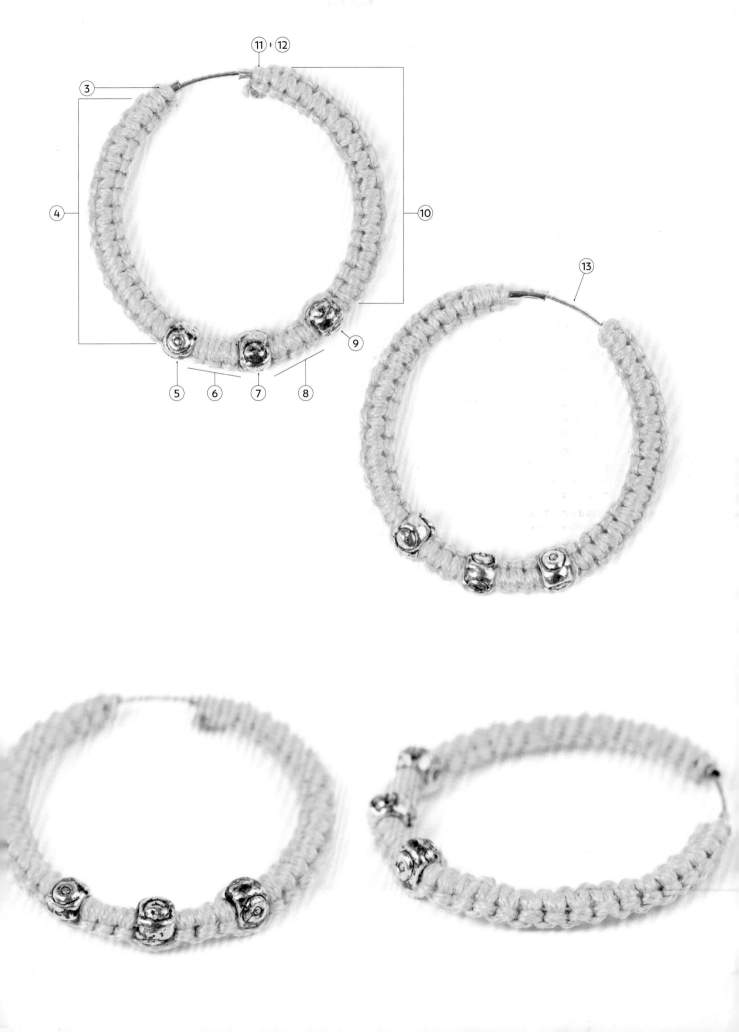

• • •

CHOKER NECKLACE

MATERIALS:

- 12m (40ft) length of 1mm (1⁄32in) nylon bead cord in a colour of your choice

- 8mm (5⁄16in) jump ring

- Fourteen 4mm (5⁄32in) round metallic beads with 2mm (3⁄32in) hole

KNOTS & TECHNIQUES:

- Reverse Lark's Head Knot

- Square Knot

- Overhand Knot

- Numbering Cords

- Plaiting

The delicate 'links' of this exquisite choker-style necklace are created using square knots embellished with metallic beads, and the finished piece is secured in place around your neck with plaited ties. Simply adjust the length of the plaits to make the necklace longer or shorter to fit. You can make a bracelet or an anklet to match your choker necklace – just tie fewer 'links'.

PREPARATION:

- Cut eight 150cm (5ft) lengths of 1mm (1⁄32in) nylon bead cord

Method

1   Secure the jump ring to the top of a project board using a T-pin (see Tools & Materials).

2   Mount four 150cm (5ft) lengths of nylon bead cord onto the jump ring with reverse lark's head knots (see Reverse Lark's Head Knot).

3   Separate the cords into two groups of four cords and tie a sinnet (see Knotting Terminology) of three square knots with each group (see Square Knot).

4   Number the cords 1 to 8 (see Numbering Cords). Thread a metal bead onto cords 4 and 5 so that the bead sits directly against the square knots above it.

5   Tie a square knot directly beneath the metal bead using cords 4 and 5 as filler cords and cords 3 and 6 as working cords (see Knotting Terminology).

6   Separate the cords into two groups of four cords and tie a sinnet of four square knots with each group.

7   Number the cords 1 to 8. Thread a metal bead onto cords 4 and 5 so that it sits directly against the square knots above it.

8   Tie a square knot directly beneath your metal bead using cords 4 and 5 as filler cords and cords 3 and 6 as working cords.

9   Repeat steps 6–8 four more times.

10   Number the cords 1 to 8. Tie an 8-cord square knot using cords 3– 6 as filler cords and cords 1 and 2 and 7 and 8 as working cords.

11   Directly beneath the 8-cord square knot, tie an overhand knot (see Overhand Knot) using all eight cords and pull really tightly to secure.

12   Cut off five of the cords just beneath the overhand knot and carefully singe the ends with a flame to melt them, taking care not to char them, then press them onto the knot.

13   With the remaining three cords, make a 12cm (4¾in) plait (see Plaiting) and tie a tight overhand knot to secure.

14   Thread a metal bead onto the cords and secure with a tight overhand knot, then trim the cords to your desired length.

15   Unpin the half-completed necklace from the project board, rotate it through 180 degrees and reattach the jump ring to the top of the project board (the completed half of the choker is still right side facing up but it is now trailing off of the top of the project board).

16   Now repeat steps 2–14 on the other side of the jump ring to complete the necklace.

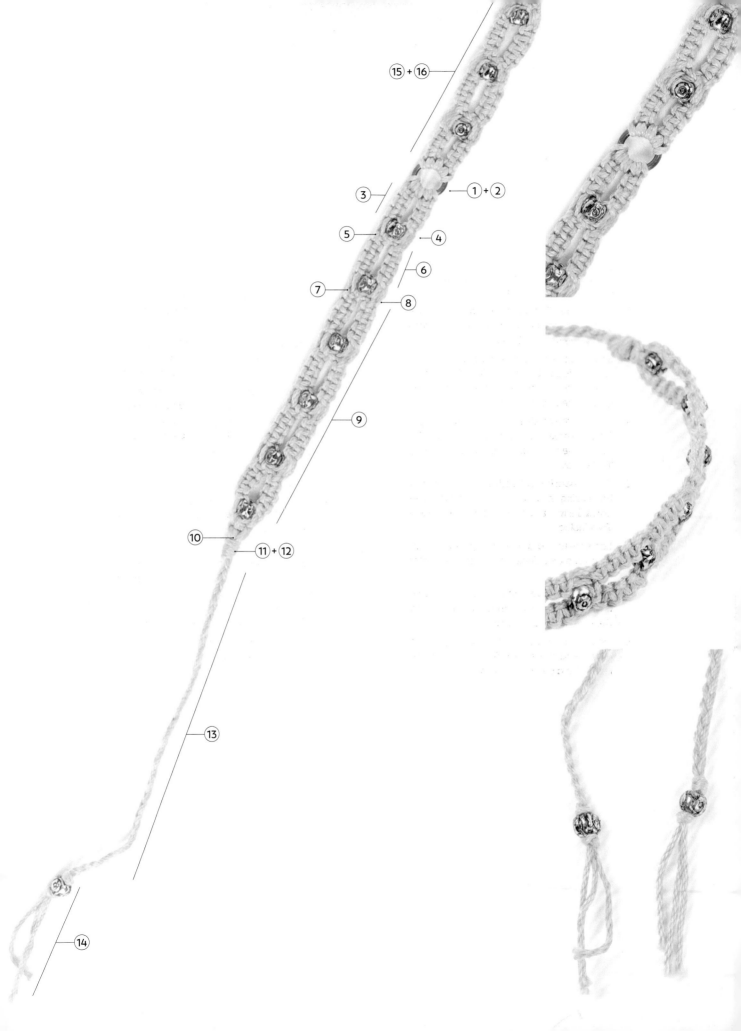

15 + 16

3

1 + 2

5

4

6

7

8

9

10

11 + 12

13

14

ABOUT THE AUTHORS

Amy Mullins and Marnia Ryan-Raison are Australian fibre artists at the forefront of the macramé movement. Sharing friendship and a love for the art of knotting, Marnia joined Amy in her online business Eden Eve in 2015. Since then, they have become two of the macramé world's leading names. Their hugely successfully online business is a place where they sell their own work as well as custom commissions, workshops and supplies, and they also offer a hire service for larger-scale pieces for special events. They have devoted themselves to creating the perfect range of modern macramé interpretations and with this, their first book, they hope to inspire and help others to achieve their dreams as macramé artists.

www.edeneve.com.au

INDEX

A SEWANDSO BOOK
© F&W Media International, Ltd 2017

SewandSo is an imprint of F&W Media International, Ltd
Pynes Hill Court, Pynes Hill, Exeter, EX2 5AZ, UK

F&W Media International, Ltd is a subsidiary of F+W
Media, Inc
10151 Carver Road, Suite #200, Blue Ash, OH 45242, USA

Text and Designs © Amy Mullins & Marnia Ryan-Raison
2017

Layout and Photography © F&W Media International,
Ltd 2017

First published in the UK and USA in 2017

A catalogue record for this book is available from the
British Library.

ISBN-13: 978-1-4463-0663-5 paperback
SRN: R5754 paperback

ISBN-13: 978-1-4463-7569-3 PDF
SRN: R5388 PDF

ISBN-13: 978-1-4463-7570-9 EPUB
SRN: R5389 EPUB

Printed in China by RR Donnelley for:
F&W Media International, Ltd
Pynes Hill Court, Pynes Hill, Exeter, EX2 5AZ, UK

10 9 8 7 6 5 4 3 2 1

Content Director: Ame Verso
Acquisitions Editor: Sarah Callard
Senior Editor: Jeni Hennah
Project Editor: Cheryl Brown
Design Manager: Anna Wade
Designer: Ali Stark
Photographer: Jason Jenkins
Art Direction: Prudence Rogers
Production Manager: Beverley Richardson

F&W Media publishes high quality books on a wide
range of subjects.
For more great book ideas visit: www.sewandso.co.uk

Layout of the digital edition of this book may vary
depending on reader hardware and display settings.